The Wreck of the Hippocampus and Other Tales of Saugatuck

by Kit Lane

Pavilion
Press
P.O. Box 250
Douglas, Mi 49406

Copyright 1992
By Pavilion Press

All Rights Reserved

ISBN 1-877703-22-2

Library of Congress Catalog Card Number
92-80010

Illustration Credits

Great Lakes Marine Collection, Milwaukee Public Library, p. 55; Fred A. Davis Collection, p. 50; drawing by Fred Stearns, p. 62; Greg Hoffman Collection, Saugatuck Douglas District Library, p. 64, 66; C. Patrick Labadie, p. 69; from Donald O. Oyler, photos taken by Ervin Diepenhorst, p. 76, 80; P. G. Walter, p. 83, 89; drawing by Sylvia Randolph, p. 96. With special thanks to Leben Productions, Saugatuck, for their technical assistance.

The cover drawing of Mount Baldhead about 1900 was done by Saugatuck artist Sylvia Randolph, with the aid of several old photographs.

Table of Contents

While the past does not change, our perception of it is altered by the evidence historians continue to uncover to document it. The recent discovery of two letters written by Saugatuck's first settler, William G. Butler, to Lucius Lyon, Congressional Representative from Michigan Territory and later a U. S. Senator, offers fresh insights into the problems and plans of the first investors in the Saugatuck area. Other letters to Lyon from visitors and settlers in Singapore and Saugatuck give an additional window into life along the Kalamazoo before 1840.

In more recent times the sad day that the Big Pavilion burned down in a spectacular fire is probably the single most-remembered day in Saugatuck history. In addition to quotations from written sources nearly a hundred residents and visitors shared their memories for this retelling and we thank them.

Over the years Saugatuck has become known as an art town, but the area seems also to have been a special inspiration to poets. Edgar Lee Masters wrote a long narrative poem containing images of Saugatuck; one of Carl Sandburg's early poetic efforts was dedicated "To Saugatuck." Greek poet George Coutoumanos lived in Saugatuck village for many years. We have included poems in two of the chapters in this book. Although neither of the poems presented here would be classed as great literature, both are good examples of the spirit of Saugatuck. They are droll, "twinkle in the eye" poetry, urging the reader not to take life -- even lawsuits -- too seriously.

Kit Lane

4

In the Shadow of Baldhead

Mount Baldhead is not really a mountain at all, but a high sand dune between the settlement of Saugatuck and Lake Michigan. In the days of man's earliest occupation of the area it was still a very active sand dune being blown eastward several feet a year. Although some grass and small shrubs have always grown on the lower slopes, in the early days there was no vegetation on the top of the dune and most of the west side, an outstanding feature which gave the hill its name.

From the beginning the dune was called Baldhead, with or without the prefix "Mount." Only outsiders, newcomers, and those waxing poetic called it "Baldy" or "Ole Baldy." References in local newspapers as early as 1878 called it Baldhead, or occasionally wrote it as two words, Bald Head. One reason for this careful terminology is a dune called Baldy on the Lake Michigan coast near Holland, just south of Lake Macatawa.

The only printed variation to what would appear to be the obvious origin of the name of the Saugatuck hill is found in *Legends of Michigan and the Old North West* written by Flavius J. Littlejohn of Allegan. The volume, according to the subtitle, is designed as: "A cluster of unpublished waifs, gleaned along the uncertain, misty line, dividing traditional from historic times." It was published in Allegan in 1875.

In one of his Native American legends that borders on the historical, Littlejohn has Wakeshma, of the local Pottawatomi tribe, and Red Wing, an ousted Sauk chief, paddle rapidly along the coast of Lake Michigan to the mouth of the Kalamazoo River, a trip the local Indian had estimated would take three hours. "Down the coast the canoe went flying with a velocity seldom witnessed. Long before the period assigned by the scout had elapsed they were rounding in to the mouth of the Kalamazoo. Up and around the Ox-bow-bend they went with unabated speed.

"Red Wing cast an occasional glance of wonder at the lofty conical sand hill known as 'Bald Eagle,' around which they were circling. Then came the expanse of the small inland lake and Saugatuck was lying before them on its margin."

In a later story, based on area involvement in the War of 1812, the same locale is seen as the home of a band of Indians headed by Chief Waukazoo. Littlejohn describes how the returning braves, "in due time, approaching the old land mark of 'Bald Eagle,' rounded in at the mouth of the Kalamazoo river, and landed at Saugatuck."

American Indians, who are less prone to baldness than their Caucasian brothers, might well have used the eagle (which has a white-feathered head making it look bald in contrast to its dark body) in their description of the sandy hilltop. Or it may have been associated with a real Bald Eagle; bald eagles still nest along the Kalamazoo. It might also have been a strictly fanciful variation added by Littlejohn.

The dune, taller than others near the mouth of the Kalamazoo River, was a gathering place for area Native American tribes from prehistoric days. It was the custom for people of this area to spend the summers in the Mackinac Island or L'Arbre Croche area. As fall approached the large summer encampments were broken up and small family groups loaded their canoes for the journey south. They would travel down Lake Michigan hugging the coast. Most would continue their travels up one of the many rivers and establish a winter camp in a stretch of forest not far from the riverbank. Each camp usually held just one Indian family, or, at most, one extended family. The surrounding territory was designed to be large enough to produce sufficient game and other food to feed the family for the winter months. In the Kalamazoo River area this usually meant that the families were far enough apart that communication with other tribal members was sporadic at best.

As spring arrived the Indians would repack and head

downstream. In later days this involved a stop at the local fur trader to receive payment for the winter's trapping, but from the earliest days the departing routine called for a stop at Mount Baldhead. According to early reporters, the Indian women and children entertained themselves at the foot of the hill while the men climbed to the top. There they performed a ritual of casting their accumulated sins on the head of a white dog brought to the top especially for this purpose. The unfortunate dog was killed, roasted, and usually eaten. Thus cleansed, the Indians were ready for another summer.

In the late 1820s, when the first white settlers arrived in western Allegan County, the area around the mouth of the Kalamazoo was controlled by a small tribe under Chief Macsaube. Some members of this tribe had fought in the War of 1812 on the British side, and the British continued to distribute presents annually. After white settlement was well underway along the Kalamazoo, the Indians arrived for the yearly ritual and displayed a large British flag at the top of the dune. Alexander Henderson and Henry Allert, described by an early historian as "captains of river flat boats," climbed the dune and seized the flag. The Indians did not resist.

Later, fire water, a foul-tasting brew concocted by the traders to make a little bit of whiskey go a long way by adding water for volume and pepper for bite, was an important part of the ritual. Jonathon Peabody, who later settled near Allegan, attended a ceremony on Baldhead in 1836 and reported: "The Indians formed a circle where they had a pail full of whiskey, and every now and then they took a dipperful and proceeded with their dance, which was a most hideous and disgusting affair, performing all sorts of gymnastics."

James Fenimore Cooper in his novel *Oak Openings*, published in 1848, used the mouth of the Kalamazoo River, projected back in time to the early 1800s, as its setting. Scholars have argued for many years about whether or not Cooper actually visited the region of Saugatuck. On the side of those

7

who feel he got no closer than Kalamazoo is the following sentence which purports to describe the land near the mouth of the river: "There was one elevated point -- elevated comparatively, if not in a very positive sense -- whence the eye could command a considerable distance along the lake shore." The shoreline, in Cooper's day as well as today, has many elevated points. Baldhead stands only slightly higher than several sand dunes nearby.

Father Jacques Marquette would have gone by the mouth of the river on his journey north following a trip to explore the Mississippi River valley in 1675. Marquette was seriously ill and there is a local tradition that he journeyed upriver, possibly as far as Allegan, seeking medical attention (he was to die before reaching St. Ignace). However, most Marquette historians feel that the tradition is unlikely to be true. It is plausible, however, that other of the early Roman Catholic missionaries visited Indians near the Kalamazoo River.

The first recorded instance of a white man visiting the area was a stop in 1820 by Gurdon Saltonstall Hubbard, a fur trader employed by John Jacob Astor's American Fur Company. He later wrote in his autobiography, "During the fall of this year I made a cache in the sandhills at the mouth of the Kalamazoo River, in which I concealed many valuables, and early in the month of March following I took one of the men and went in a canoe for the articles. We found everything safe and in good condition, and having loaded them into the canoe started home."

Although the top of Baldhead and parts of the west face were bare well into the 20th Century, most of the lower reaches, the east slope and base have always been heavily wooded. Parts of the forest on the northwest slope of Baldhead, and in the area between Baldhead and Lone Pine (the next hill to the north where the Saugatuck water reservoir was later built) are said to be virgin timber. The towering trees were left because of the difficulties of cutting and transporting logs in the steep sand. These protected areas also have an abundance of wild flowers, including many varieties of trillium in the springtime, jack-in-the-pulpit, and phlox. Birds migrating along the Great Lakes flyway are frequent visitors in the spring and fall, and several species also nest on the slopes. Deer are often seen, especially in the early evening on the lake side, and foxes, raccoons, squirrels and other small rodents are abundant.

May Francis Heath, in *Early Memories of Saugatuck*, prints part of the memoirs left by her grandmother, early schoolteacher Mary Elizabeth Peckham, who married Stephen A. Morrison, an early Saugatuck tanner and postmaster. The story she relates took place some time between Mary Elizabeth's marriage to Morrison in 1840 and Constance Bingham's marriage to George Jewett in 1855.

"One time Constance Bingham came to visit me during her vacation from teaching in the Loomis School. She had always had a great desire to climb Mt. Baldhead, which was then in the midst of a dense wilderness, with a narrow path to its base from the ferry. I was not able to accompany her so she decided bravely to go alone. The ferry man rowed her across the Kalamazoo and directed her how to go, and after several attempts she at last reached the top. After enjoying the scenery awhile she went down the other side of the lake and stumbled on a little Indian mound where an Indian child had been buried. She gathered wild flowers and made wreaths with which she adorned the little grave. She rested a while, then began the long climb up the west side of Baldhead, finally reaching the top, and sat musing over the incident of the Indian grave and weaving a story about it to tell her pupils at school Monday morning. While thus occupied the bushes beside her began to crack

9

and snap and a black 'something' thrust its head through the branches and gave an ugly grunt. Constance, too startled to even look back -- for whatever it be cows or bears 'twas all the same to her, with well directed bounds lost no time in getting to the foot of Baldhead. She was terribly frightened, imagining all the animals of the forest were chasing her, so she ran at high speed to the ferry, arriving there in such a shaking and frightened state she could not speak, and the kind old ferryman told her she was coming down with 'Michigan ague' and he advised her to get home as soon as possible and take plenty of quinine. He did not need to urge her to hurry, for hurry she did, and finally reached my home and my arms, and, quivering with excitement she told the story of her adventure. And in the morning Mr. Morrison started out with a party of men who finally found and killed in the woods near Baldhead a large Black Bear, the largest ever seen in these parts, and Constance, the school ma'am, had a real story to tell her pupils for she was quite the heroine of the day."

The high sand dune was a favorite scene for writers of fiction. Michigan author Bruce Catton is said to have used Baldhead as a scene in his Civil War novel for juveniles, *Banners at Shenandoah*. In the early pages of the book, the young boy who narrates the story, actually too young to enlist in the war, runs off to do just that. He leaves his uncle a note and climbs up to the top of a nearby dune to hide until he can make his escape in the dark of night. As he waits for sunset, the boy relaxes in a small grove of pine trees. He later describes the scene, "It was nice up there. The bluff was at least three hundred feet high, and very steep. You could see for miles up and down the big blue lake, with the yellow sand running along the shore as far as you could see . . ."

"OLD BALD HEAD,"

Or, Six Months In a Hunters' Camp.

By Prof. H. T. Trowber.

1. The Kalamazoo river eastern foot of "Bald Head."

2. "Old Bald Head," eastern slope. Commencing the ascent.

3. Lake Michigan, western foot of "Bald Head." Lighthouse at mouth of Kalamazoo river.

The wonderful two thousand dollar prize story of pioneer life in Western Michigan; full of illustrations, adventures, and descriptions of the beautiful scenery along the Kalamazoo river and Lake Michigan.

Regular edition $1.50, cloth bound. We are just issuing a limited paper bound edition of the story, complete and unabridged. If you want a copy of the cheap edition, send 50 cents at once to The Educator Publishing Co., Battle Creek, Mich., and receive it by mail, postpaid.

Galveston News:—The opening chapters of "Old Bald Head," or Six Months in a Hunters' Camp, contains the finest description of a storm we have ever seen. This is the story that created such a contest among publishers for its possession. The author, Prof. H. T. Trowber, a former brother journalist, finally accepted $2,000 in cash and a royalty on every copy sold. The young people of the country are fortunate in having this thrilling story of adventure added to their literature.

The Commercial's Great Offer

FOR THE NEXT THIRTY DAYS we will send the above story, complete, to any one who will renew their subscription to the COMMERCIAL for one year.

Address THE LAKE SHORE COMMERCIAL, SAUGATUCK, MICH.

Mount Baldhead was also the setting for a boys adventure story, *Old Baldhead, or, Six Months in a Hunters' Camp*. This tale was printed as a pulp novel and given away free in 1896 with new subscriptions to the *Lake Shore Commercial*, Saugatuck's weekly newspaper. In more recent years the dunes near the shore have been the setting for two children's novels, *Potawatomi Indian Summer* published in 1975, written by E. William Oldenberg, and *White Mist* written in 1985 by Barbara Smucker.

In the opening chapter of Arnold Mulder's 1921 book *The Sand Doctor*, the place where the lovers meet is clearly Saugatuck although the names are changed. "In the middle of the afternoon he climbed to the top of the Crowned Monarch. . . He would have a good look around -- the dunes to the north, over Finley to the south, over the Big Swamp and the Larramore Farms beyond to the east, and over the lake to the west. . . But of the dunes he was hardly conscious; and the lake -- locally known as the 'big lake' to distinguish it from the river which was almost a bay -- was only a body of water." A contemporary literary critic wrote "although the setting is a blurred composite of the east shore of Lake Michigan that the first meeting of the lovers occurs on Mount Baldhead is clear, however, for no other part of the shore fits the description and the fate of Singapore doubtless is suggested in the buried city in the novel."

According to the two-volume *History of the Great Lakes* published in 1899, Saugatuck is part of the setting of a book written in 1874 by E. P. Roe, then a popular novelist. The story of *Opening a Chestnut Burr* brings the main character back to his home town, although there is nothing that would make it specifically Saugatuck or even Michigan to the modern eye.

Climbing the dune, especially before the first stairs were built, has always been a physical feat to reckon with. As early as 1870 it was regarded as a challenge, and in June of that year the *Saugatuck Commercial* carried the following news:

The Allegan *Journal* says the Fat Men's Association of Allegan is coming down the river to Saugatuck to bathe in the waters and sniff the fresh breezes of Lake Michigan. They have voted to mount 'Baldhead,' the highest and nearly perpendicular bluff at the entrance of the Kalamazoo River into Lake Michigan. The members of the F. M. A. have sworn in their associated capacity, that they shall climb this hill and roll on the fine, beautiful sand of 'bald head' or die in the attempt! We admire the noble resolutions of the F. M. A., for that body is composed of men of spirit and determination. The weather is hot and an ascension of 'bald head' fatiguing and exhaustive in its character, particularly during the sultry weather.

We would advise the Village Marshal, Smalley, and that honorable and august body -- the Saugatuck Common Council -- to make ample arrangements for the reception of the ponderosities of Allegan County and that they be treated with due consideration becoming men of their weight. . ."

When it became apparent that the first railroad built on the Lake Michigan shore would run east of the settlement the Saugatuck Village Council began looking for other means to satisfy the transportation needs of area business. The solution they agreed on was a proposal to deed the dune and the area surrounding it to any railroad which would build a line that passed through or terminated within the boundaries of the village. After many paper promises, one railroad, the Columbus, Lima and Milwaukee, actually began construction of a track, and, with great ceremony and optimism, a one-half interest in Baldhead was deeded to promoter B. C. Faurot.

The track begun by the line near Lima, Ohio, never

13

even got as far north as the Ohio-Michigan line and the Village of Saugatuck began the long legal process to reclaim the deed from the promoter and develop the high dune itself and the area at its base into Mount Baldhead Park, including a community of summer cottages, a pavilion for picnics and meetings and a tent camp.

Following the grand opening of the new park, the local newspaper boasted in the August 22, 1884, issue: "A large number of the villagers did the new park Sunday afternoon and expressed themselves delighted with the same, wondering at the great change that was made in so short a time. Brethren of the press are invited to come down and take a look at Saugatuck, its Baldhead Park and the race course. They will not have to be asked to give it a puff, for we know they can't help themselves."

The following week volunteers spread many wagon loads of sawdust on the roads along the west bank of the river, and subscriptions were taken "to build an observatory on the crest of Baldhead so that persons can have an unobstructed view of the country from all points of the compass." The members of the Douglas Band puffed their way to the top and "rendered some excellent music. It was very distinct and must have been heard a long distance off."

The tower was quickly completed. The newspaper of September 12, 1884, described it. "The observatory on the crest of Baldhead is forty feet higher than the top of the hill, giving an unobstructed view of the country in every direction. A flag staff forty feet in height will be placed upon this, and a Chicagoan who went into ecstacies of delight when he reached the top has agreed to send over a flag worthy of the park enterprise." It was unfurled on October 21, and the newspaper reported "the heavens wept for joy -- it rained for ten hours."

As part of the celebration the village council offered to pay the wedding fees for the first couple to get married on the top of Baldhead. On September 17, 1884, John E. Reed and

Miss Hattie M. Beagle of Fennville climbed to the top and were married by the Rev. W. D. Attack.

Winds on top of Baldhead can be fierce, and the observatory blew down in 80 mile-per-hour gusts during a storm in December of 1888, but was rebuilt a few weeks later at the cost of $40.

In the spring of 1886 the village built an outdoor pavilion at the foot of the hill on the tree-shaded eastern side near the river. It quickly became a popular gathering place for Sunday School picnics. In 1893 the pavilion was the focus of the Allegan County Soldiers and Sailors Reunion, drawing 200 Union Army veterans and a total crowd of more than 3,000.

On several occasions there was discussion about the name of the tall hill. In 1889 the editor of the *Saugatuck Commercial* wrote, "It is a growing impression that the park which lends its value to this place as a summer resort, has not a poetical name; and this very thing, let it be known, is a chief essential to a successful summering place. 'Baldhead' dear as the name is to those who have lived within sight of the gleaming crown of the old hill, sounds unfine when compared with Macatawa, Ottawa Beach, Highland Park, Interlaken and so on. The famous resorts of the East, it will be noted, have flourished under names that charm the ear, such as Saratoga, Long Branch, Bar Harbor -- the latter brings a suggestion; we have a harbor, the harbor has a bar, so there is nothing to bar our adopting the name. What say you citizens, to the rechristening?"

An earlier quest for a new name brought the suggestions Ki-kal-ma-zu (accent on the last syllable) Nim-mee-kee, after a chief of the Ottawa tribe who was born, lived, and died on the banks of the Kalamazoo, and "several modern names." It was decided to retain the name Baldhead "since it is known by that title everywhere along the chain of lakes."

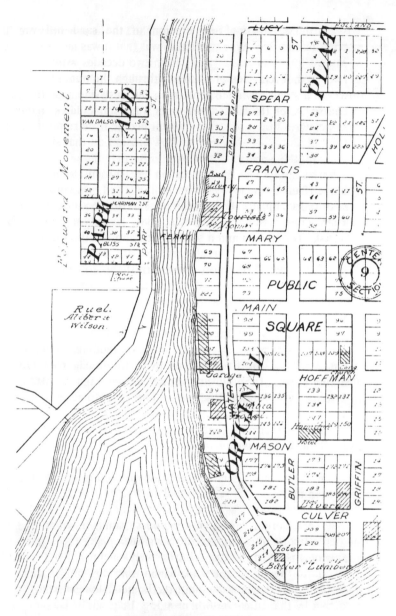

Map of the Park Addition

16

The drifting and erosion of the sand hill was a continuing worry. One prediction was that it was moving at the rate of four feet a year and within two decades would fill the river bed, forcing the river to cut through the dunes, probably where a small creek still enters on the west side near the golf course. After the first set of stairs was completed on the east slope, wires were erected to prevent people from running down the hill alongside the steps to slow erosion on that side.

A plan to grow trees on the summit to lessen the blowing of the sand was tried in 1887, and was considered a failure, but apparently some trees survived because a second assessment in the September 20, 1889, *Saugatuck Commercial* noted, "The trees planted by the village authorities on the crest of Baldhead two or three years ago, are nearly all alive and growing finely. The object was to arrest the drifting sand over the top of the hill and if the system is carried out it will accomplish this result."

Fences built atop the hill in 1895 slowed the drifting of the sand somewhat, and are credited with adding seven feet to the dune's height In March of 1896 the official government survey showed that the summit was 226 feet high. By March of 1897, it was reported that the 10-foot fences had been nearly buried beneath the sand. "They have increased the altitude of the hill that much, and so far have arrested the further movement of sand toward the river."

As both a money-raising scheme and to encourage the growth of Saugatuck as a summer resort, the Village Council in 1894 voted to have a series of lots platted near the foot of Mt. Baldhead and sold for the erection of summer cottages. The December 7, 1894 issue of the Saugatuck paper explained that the lots may be procured in the following manner: "On payment of $25 to the village clerk a contract will be given calling for a deed to the lot selected as soon as the purchaser has completed a dwelling thereon costing not less than $150. In event no dwelling is built within a year from the date thereof the contract will become void. This latter provision is to prevent the lots from falling into the hands of those who wish to hold them for speculative purposes only. The council also passed a resolution creating a park improvement fund and directing that all sums received from the sale of park lots should be used for park improvement purposes only."

The first cottages built were constructed by local people, apparently primarily for the rental trade. The April 12, 1895, paper noted that "building operations on the first cottage to be erected in Baldhead park will begin in a few days. A. Houtkamp will be the owner and it will occupy a sightly location just south of Mt. Baldhead and a few rods from the river." Houtkamp was then editor of the newspaper. The following week the paper recorded that Frank Kirby, E. E. Weed and F. M. Weed, all prominent local businessmen, were negotiating for purchase of two park lots, with a view of building three or possibly four cottages. The writer (probably Houtkamp) went on to observe, "The site they have selected is one of the finest of the park grounds and they stand a good chance of realizing a handsome profit on their investment. It is morally certain that park lots will never again be sold so cheap as they are this season and before many years they will be in good demand at fancy prices. Some of our local capitalists would do well to take advantage of the present opportunity."

A new dock was built at the park grounds to facilitate the movement of goods and furniture, and by the summer of 1898 there were nine cottages already built, and two more under construction. Tenting became popular near the end of the 19th Century, and a number of visitors erected large tents north of the pavilion at the foot of Baldhead. In the spring of 1897 the village passed an ordinance to charge $1 per tent per week. There was a protest and a petition circulated to repeal the charge. In the March 26, 1897 issue, the *Lake Shore Commercial* defended the new rules. "The ordinance is both necessary and just and will not be detrimental to the development of the park. Its passage was requested by several campers from Chicago who occupied the park lands last season, and it was with them, in fact, that the idea originated. The village is at considerable expense each year in improving and maintaining the park grounds and property and it is not unjust to ask those for whose benefit these improvements are made to help bear the burden. Enough revenue should be derived from the rental of the park lands to keep a watchman on the grounds night and day during the resort season, and this can probably easily be done if the ordinance is allowed to remain in force."

The following month the ordinance was amended to reduce the fee from $1 per week to $1 per month. The editor sighed, "There is little inducement for people to buy lots and build cottages where tenting privileges can be procured so cheaply."

Many of the tents were far from roughing it. They were usually large wall tents, accommodating a full family. Many of them had permanent wooden floors, often with rugs, comfortable chairs, and cots for sleeping. Some of the tents were also rigged with running water. Sometimes a large group would rent two tents, one for sleeping and the other for dining. Some cooking was done in fireplaces, but the campers also frequently crossed on the ferry to dine at boarding houses and later in restaurants in Saugatuck.

Despite the competition from the tents six more lots were sold in 1898, two in 1899, and the last in 1903 when it was reported "The city has sold 44 park lots since 1896. About the first 20 to 25 were sold for $25 each, the title not being perfectly clear. Then the title was cleared up and the remaining lots were sold for $50 each."

In 1904 the village council entertained a proposal by C. M. Cook for a 300-room, four-story hotel to be built on top of Baldhead but wisely declined to transfer the deed to the developer until the hotel was completed. It was never begun.

Shifting sand continued to be a frightening problem. By 1900 the stairs on the east slope had been completely covered and in the May 26, 1905, issue of the *Commercial Record* an article warned, "The eastward movement of Mount Baldhead must be stopped before its encroachment upon the river interferes with navigation."

In June J. M. Westgate erected two parallel fences crosswise of the west slope of the hill and set out grass on the top and west slope. Brush was scattered to give the plantings some stability. The following spring the newspaper reported, "The plan laid out by the Department of Agriculture to stop the shifting sands of Mt. Baldhead has not met with complete success nor is it a failure. The grass seed was planted in rows extending south from the old tower . . . that on higher ground is more exposed than the other and in some places killed by freezing. The variety of grass that was transplanted seems to be growing all right in most places and the sand fences have done good work. The thing that has caused the most damage is the sliding down of the sand caused by people climbing the hill; in some places the plank walk between Mt. Baldhead and Lone Pine is already covered with sand."

In 1913 Bessie Ruel, who would later become one of the first women in the country to be ordained a Methodist pastor, began a campaign to build a new set of stairs up the side of the hill to eliminate the erosion caused by climbing in the soft sand. The paper reported, "She has sent for 100 small contribution boxes which are to be distributed among the resorts and be in charge of young ladies who will see that they are not overlooked. The money will be taken out from time to time and left in charge of Mr. Takken at the bank." The August 1, 1913, *Commercial Record* had a few other suggestions, "The proposed stairway would keep people from climbing the steep hillside, but probably a cog railway would be more popular if someone could be induced to invest the necessary money in it. It has been suggested that a refreshment stand would pay, for there is always a demand for cool and refreshing drinks after one reaches the summit of Baldhead."

Money came in slowly for the new stairs, and in a November storm in 1916 the tower at the top of Baldhead was blown down. It had been considered unsafe to climb for several years (though individuals undoubtedly did climb it), but its collapse was unexpected. In 1925 the area behind the village's pumping station on the Kalamazoo River was filled with sand to make a more level area at the base of the big dune. This had the effect of leaving the slate roof of the red brick pumping station at the ground level of the park and pavilion. The pumphouse and generating plant had been built in the late 1890s to provide electric power for the Village of Saugatuck as well as for the pumping of the water supply. In 1901 a water reservoir had been built into the summit of nearby Lone Pine, the next dune to the north. The power station operated for only a short time until Saugatuck tied into Consumers Power network, but the building continued in use many years as a pumping station for the water supply.

The old observation tower

One of the fondest memories many resorters and residents have of Baldhead is the "swinging vine." It would appear that there have been several. The first was apparently a true vine on the east side of the dune about where the stairs were later built. It was a short swing but seemed longer because of the steep incline which left the swinger with a ten to fifteen foot drop into the soft sand, adding greatly to the erosion problems. The fragile vine was later replaced with a sturdier rope. The last rope swing existed as recently as the mid-1970s on the south slope.

Tenting in the area continued. One of the popular fixtures of the campground was Chief Blue Sky, an Indian from South Dakota, who would (for a fee) stage a pow-wow complete with dancing and the smoking of the peace pipe. In 1925 he was hired as a deputy marshal and caretaker of Baldhead Park. The local newspaper commented, "The Chief now wears a smile of contentment and a shining star of authority."

By 1931 a new staircase of 367 steps had been completed to the summit of the hill, and the road on the west side of the river had been widened and graveled, "ample width for safety." Efforts continued to make Baldhead stand still. The April 15, 1932, issue of the *Commercial Record* reported:

"Work has been resumed on the top and west side of Mount Baldhead. Men are busy cutting brush and spreading it; willow and locust saplings are being planted and rye sown to keep the sand from blowing away. The work is being done under the direction of Harry Newnham.

"Since this conservation project was started about a year ago, it has received widespread attention. Detailed reports have been requested and sent to the conservation department and a number of people interested in this work have been here to inspect it. Mr.

22

Kroodsma, extension forester, of Michigan State College at East Lansing, has cooperated with our village conservation chairman, Mr. August Pfaff, in getting this work started. "Tuesday of this week three young men, natives of Brazil and students of Michigan University Forestry Department, were here to get information about the work. They were greatly interested.

"Old Baldhead being Saugatuck's greatest natural attraction, brings people from far and near to our village and is deserving of all the attention it is receiving. To realize this all one need do is to climb to the top and be rewarded with the wonderful view from there. No effort should be spared in preserving this priceless landmark."

In the spring of 1939 the Park Commission of the Village of Saugatuck planted 6,000 red and jack pines on the back of Baldhead, and 100 walnut trees and flowering tulip trees on the river side. The following year there was a proposal to build a 60 foot steel observatory at the summit. (Ten feet taller than the 50 foot tower in the Irish Hills.) However, plans were interrupted by World War II and never revived.

In 1940 an outdoor stove was built by Harry Newnham at the small park at the foot of the stairs. In 1944 the pavilion was refurbished, and the old wood floor was replaced with concrete. The roof was also lowered two feet to improve its qualities as a rain shelter.

Following World War II, and especially after the Korean conflict began in 1951, there was concern that the Soviet Union or other Eastern Hemisphere enemies might attempt to attack the United States with planes flying over the North Pole. To guard against this possibility the Air Force created the Distant Early Warning (DEW) Line, and erected a

23

station at the top of Mount Baldhead, designated the Saugatuck Gap Filler Annex PIN 5521.

The station consisted of a 75-foot high tower with a revolving radar dish attached and a small blockhouse filled with radar and weather detection devices. In 1964 the radar apparatus was enclosed in a fiberglass bubble to provide the men performing maintenance and repairs on the machinery with some shield against the high winds on the summit.

The site for the station was leased from the Village of Saugatuck and sturdily fenced. Part of the agreement called for the Air Force to build a new set of stairs up to the summit which would be available to all. During construction a track was laid alongside the new staircase to carry construction material up the side of the dune. There was also a water line and a line carrying fuel oil from a tank near the foot of the stairs running up the hill to supply the blockhouse.

For a time after the radar unit went on line the Air Force had several men from an Air Force maintenance unit at Fort Custer near Battle Creek stationed fulltime in Saugatuck to man and maintain the installation. However, an officer explained later, "The daily climb finally got to them, and they were seldom at the top as they were supposed to be, so we had the base put on fully automatic operation."

By 1968 new planes and detection devices had made the station obsolete and it was deactivated. That summer it was declared surplus property and purchased by the Village of Saugatuck for $250, with no particular plans, but with a view toward retaining the large white-domed tower which had become a landmark. After a short-lived skirmish with the Air Force, which had not been notified of the sale and tried to remove the radar equipment, the village took over care of the site, probably the only village in the country with its own radar installation.

24

At least once under village ownership the radar apparatus was activated. As the big dish rotated inside the dome, viewers at the controls in the blockhouse at the foot of the tower gazed at the radar screen. It revealed no Russian bombers, but a flotilla of sailboats racing near Holland, fishing boats trolling near Saugatuck, and an occasional private plane flying along the coast.

In the early 1970s the tower was used as a radiotelephone station for ship-to-shore communications. Also, beginning about 1967, the tower base is adorned with an electrically lighted star each Christmas season.

In 1973 the old pumphouse, no longer in use, was leased to a private individual for use as a cottage. It was at this time that the slate roof was removed.

The efforts of the conservationists had been rewarded and by 1970 the movement of the dune had been stabilized by plantings on the sides and top. However, the cost was obstruction of the view. Those who completed the climb up the Air Force stairway could look directly down the stairway to the river and down a narrow path on the west side to the lake, but foliage and trees blocked all other views.

In 1976, with encouragement and some financial help from the Saugatuck Township Park Commission, a master plan for Mount Baldhead was developed and some improvements, including a fishing dock, and some marked trails, were completed. Grants were received to help complete the plan which included $27,570 as the projected cost of a stairway and overlook near the river and an overlook at the summit giving the climber, once again, a view of Saugatuck Village, Douglas Village and a look up the Kalamazoo River unobstructed by the trees at that top.

BALDHEAD

(Reprinted from the March 9, 1878, Allegan Journal)

Said two pert young misses, one morning, "Good morning, grandpapa, let's take a walk."

"Well where shall we go?"

"Why, on the top of Baldhead, of course! We were never there, never in all our lives."

"But I am getting old and Baldhead is very steep and high: and how can I climb up there?"

"Oh, we will help you up -- one take hold of each hand and pull, and pull, until we get you up there some way."

And now here we are, after a great deal of hard work, right on the topmost point of it. It is all sand here, not a speck of dirt -- nothing but the cleanest and whitest sand. No new-born snow was ever purer or whiter; you can sit right down on it and rest yourselves, and not soil your clothes in the least. O, what a splendid prospect! How beautiful! Why, we can see miles and miles on lake Michigan and here are the light-houses and piers, and mouth of the river, right at our feet on one side; and Kalamazoo lake and river, and Saugatuck and Douglas and a grand expanse of country rolling off to meet the sky on the other. How small things look down there -- the steamboats look like tugs, the vessels like fishboats, the horses like ponies, and the men like the queer folks Gulliver tells about.

I dare say it is not all of the residents of the Kalamazoo Valley, or all of the readers of The Journal, that have ever been on the top of Baldhead -- perhaps some of them have never even heard of him. For the benefit of such we will say that Baldhead is one of the most noted headlands in southern Michigan. The world has thousands of more grand and majestic scenes that he can unfold to the visitor, but few that are more variegated, charming, and lovely. He stands right in the gateway of the Kalamazoo river, as it discharges its waters into lake Michigan, and says, with a grand bow -- for recollect, we are always on fairy ground when up here. "Good morning, Mrs. Kalamazoo river. How do you do? And how are your children and grandchildren, the beautiful towns and villages you have planted on your way here?" "Quite well, I thank you, all except Miss Kalla, who is getting a little old maidish and quite jealous of Miss Battle Creek since she had learned that father W--- has promised her that dashing young spark the Michigan Ship Canal with all the commerce of the world for her dowry." "Well, Mrs. Kalamazoo, I have been expecting you a long time. I could see your roadway at a great distance from here, and have noticed your progress as you wound your way down through the forest, and this morning, as soon as it was light, I caught the first glimpse of your lovely face in the distance, and have been admiring your graceful curves and meanderings ever since. I know your destination, that you are on a journey to meet your mother who is on the other side of me -- and that I stand in your way. I am old; I beg your pardon, madam, but it is hard work for me to move." So she dropped him a curtsey and swept gracefully around him and was lost in the waters of the great lake. See how different they look when they first meet each other -- how gradually but perfectly they blend together until mother and daughter become one body.

But the wind is coming up and the sea making fast. How it rolls on the beach and pounds against the piers and breaks over them; and see the whitecaps rising and falling in the distance. "O grandpapa! What are those white-looking things away off on the water?" "They are large vessels loaded with the commerce of the world -- some going one way, some another; some with the wind, some beating up against it. They roll and pitch and plunge with the sea. But up here we are on enchanted ground. They look like ghosts have a grand masquerade. We will call them the Miss Phantoms. See how grandly they bow to each other -- what a handsome curtsey Miss Fanny Phantom drops her sister Miss Flora, as she comes about to take the other tack. Ladies cross over -- all hand around -- promenade all! and away they go to their several ports of destination."

"What is that black streak away beyond the Miss Phantoms, with the white specks behind it?" "That is the large tug Leviathan with her tow of barges loaded with lumber bound for Chicago."

Now we will turn around and take a peep at Saugatuck and then go home. Be careful my good friends of the village how you act now. We can look down on you -- we can see every little street and alley and crooked place in your town, and as we are on enchanted ground we can almost see your very hearts and motives and interpret your conduct. There is the spot where Santa Claus unloads his toys when on a visit to his children; and there are the cunning little holes he crawls into when he goes below to fill their stockings with good things. There comes young Slyboots out of his father's house into the back yard, and there is Miss Modesty just over the fence in her mother's garden. See how they edge up to it behind the grapevine. Smack! Oh, George! you naughty boy! I didn't think you would do that again. Never mind, your mamma didn't see you. Well, we did. Don't think you can hide such work from us up here.

Yonder goes Mr. Thirsty Fellow to the dram shop. He is so dry he can't stand it any longer, and his sick wife is drawing a pail of water from a deep well with nothing but a clothes-line. And there goes Worthless to the billiard table. He must have exercise -- he can;t live without it, and his wife is in the back yard splitting wood. Look at the garden

27

of Old Mope. He loves vegetables -- how good they look in his neighbor's garden; but his garden -- ah, the weeds turned his garden out of doors long ago.

But -- but what? I guess I have been asleep. It is nothing but a dream. Not all -- there stands glorious old Baldhead, the hero of a thousand years, firm, erect, facing the great lake and all the storms it can marshal forth, venerable in years and hoary with age, at once the glory and protection of Saugatuck. Saugatuckians don't half appreciate him. He is too familiar with you. He greets you in the morning with a smile and signals the last news of the setting sun.

Go often to visit him -- go with a tender heart and right mind. See how he will unfold the beauties of nature to your vision. Stand on his peak and turn slowly around. How majestically he unrolls the map of your country and wafts it away. A thousand square miles of the earth's surface, beautifully diversified with land and water, are spread out there and roll away beyond the reach of sight. There you can mark the improvements that are taking place each year around you. New farms come forth from their hiding places in the wilderness, at the bidding of industry; orchards and gardens, and cottages spring up like magic and are photographed there in the twinkling of an eye. Strangers come often to visit him and are sure to go away charmed and instructed, and always with the hope and determination of visiting him again. This will always be the case with every true lover of nature.

T. G.

CAMPING GROUNDS, SAUGATUCK, MICH.

28

"What's in a Name?"

Placenames did not come easily to the settlers of Western Allegan County. Some of their choices were already taken; others were later usurped by more ambitious projects elsewhere. Nearly every community can claim at least two names in its history and some have been known by as many as five.

The first settler in what would later be called Saugatuck was William G. Butler, of Hartford, Connecticut, via Elkhart, Indiana, who had arrived at the mouth of the Kalamazoo River in 1829 to locate a homesite and trading post. In 1830 he built a home on the flat piece of land about two miles upriver where a village would shortly be platted. As a result of his settlement he was permitted to enter a large tract as a pre-emption, land on which he was allowed first choice because he was already living there and had made improvements.

In 1833, when the rest of the land around was opened up for purchase, he sought cash so that he could make additional purchases. His father sent him $500 to invest, and he sold half of his pre-emption to a company formed by John Griffith of New York, of the house of "J & E G," proprietors of the Troy & Erie Line, who was living in St. Joseph, Col. S. E. Mason and Henry B. Hoffman of Niles and himself. These four met the day of the sale, formed the company, and agreed to call the settlement that Butler had begun by the name of **Newark**. (The main business street in Saugatuck is called Butler, and three downtown cross streets Hoffman, Mason and Griffith still commemorate the original investors.)

Why they chose this name is not recorded. The most obvious source for the name is the settlement of Newark in New Jersey which had been established before 1700, but there is also a Newark in New York State, not far from Albany, one in northwestern Connecticut, and one in Ohio.

However, although the township officially took the name Newark, a plat of the settlement that was recorded in 1834 gave it the name of **Kalamazoo**, taken from the river. The name Kalamazoo is an Indian word and has been variously translated. The most commonly cited origin and translation, and the one mentioned on the roadside marker on the interstate highway south of the present-day City of Kalamazoo, is that it is from a Miami Indian word variously written *ke-kanamazoo* and *ke-kal-ima-zoo*, meaning "boiling water." Expounders of this theory further explain that the boiling water was mentioned because:

1. The eddies in the rapids of the river often resemble boiling water.

2. Boiling was a favorite recipe of the cannibalistic tribes along the river for cooking their victims.

3. The Pottawatomi tribe would sometimes gather and run a footrace. The winner was the brave who could cover a specified distance the largest number of times before a pot of water boiled on the fire.

Henry Rowe Schoolcraft wrote that Kalamazoo was from *negikanamazoo* which he describes variously as meaning "otters beneath the surface" and "water running over the rocks that on reflection looks like otters." One version, supported by Father Verwyst and W. R. Gerard, describes Kalamazoo as an alteration of the Chippewa word *kikalamoza* meaning "he is inconvenienced by smoke in his lodge."

Virgil J. Vogel, in *Indian Names in Michigan* published by the University of Michigan Press in 1986, says there is no certain derivation of the name. He writes that it may be a variation on the Chippewa word *kikikamagad*, "it goes or runs fast," or a mangled form of *kalimink* or *killomick*, which have been interpreted to mean "deep still water." Both names describe the Kalamazoo River at various places along its length.

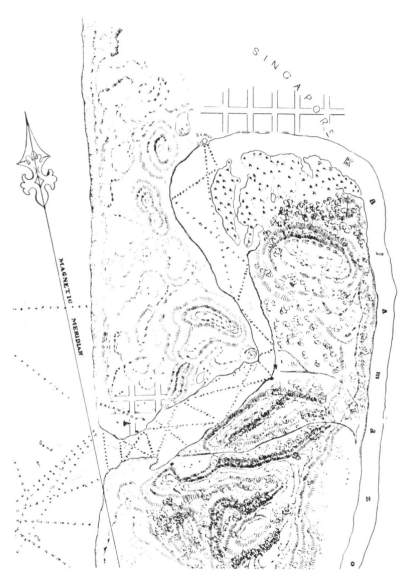

A detail from the 1844 map shows "Kalamazoo" near the lighthouse at left, and two paths through the woods towards Saugatuck which was across the river on the right.

Why the plat was recorded as Kalamazoo is a mystery. Thomas Fitzgerald of St. Joseph, a friend of Griffith, wrote that the group had decided the day of the purchase "upon Newark as its permanent name, and that the plat would be recorded by that name." Butler, in a letter written December 20, 1833, advises a correspondent to address his reply to "Newark, Allegan P. Office M.T." [Michigan Territory].

A letter from H. H. Comstock, who owned the land at the mouth of the river, to Lucius Lyon, their territorial delegate in Congress, written Christmas Day, 1833, states "Messrs. Griffith, Butler & Hoffman requested me to ask of you to make an application to the post office department for a post office to be located at Newark (the name they have given to the place)."

In addition to the settlement on Kalamazoo Lake, Butler and his business partners had plans to erect a warehouse farther down the river near the mouth, and, according to a later letter by Butler, to dig a canal which would connect the warehouse near the mouth with the settlement. An 1844 engineer's map shows a trail to a warehouse located about where the Ox-Bow Summer School of Painting developed later, and the most obvious route for a canal would be just south of the road.

The 1844 map also shows another source for confusion, a second settlement which was platted about the same time as Kalamazoo/Newark/Saugatuck, at the mouth of the Kalamazoo River, just east of the lighthouse. The nucleus of the settlement was to be a warehouse for the transfer of river cargo to lake boats owned by Stephen Nichols, who was also the lighthouse keeper. This projected settlement on the 1844 map contains only four streets and is labeled **Kalamazoo**.

To add to the confusion the original plat of Allegan County's Kalamazoo (later Saugatuck) was lost. It was stolen, a newspaper story reports, in the late 1890s by a woman impersonating a clerk, who hoped to hold it for ransom. It was never ransomed, and Stephen A. Morrison, who had a hand in the original map, attempted to reconstruct it later from field notes which he had retained.

There seems to be little argument that the official plat of the town was called Kalamazoo, and thus that would have been the legal name of the settlement. In 1836 settlers in the town of Bronson in Kalamazoo County wanted to change its name, possibly to distance themselves a little from their founder, Titus Bronson, described by historians as "an honest but eccentric" individual. Their choice for a new name was Kalamazoo, the name of the river on which the settlement was founded. They were unaware, or took no notice, that the name Kalamazoo was already taken. An 1838 Michigan gazetteer beneath the heading Newark wrote:

Saugatuc post office, Allegan county, on the Michigan city and Grand Haven post route. (See Newark.)

Newark, (called Kalamazoo on the maps,) is a village and post office, in a township of the same name, in the county of Allegan. It is located about two miles from Lake Michigan, on the Kalamazoo river. There is a steam saw mill building, and a warehouse already constructed. It numbers perhaps 10 or 12 dwellings. The location of this place is eligible, and the harbor commodious ; and there is a prospect of its becoming a place of importance. Distant 21 miles from Allegan, and 180 from Detroit.

One of the reasons that the Bronson-Kalamazoo name-changers were apparently unaware of another town named Kalamazoo in Allegan County was that there was never a post office by that name in the county. The post office that was called Kalamazoo was established in Calhoun County on May 2, 1834, with Reuben Abbott as the first postmaster. He had arrived in the southwestern corner of Calhoun County and built a tavern on the road to Marshall, near where Albion was later organized. This settlement was near the Kalamazoo River, and took the name of the river. It was later a station on the

Michigan Central Railroad. The name of the post office of Kalamazoo, Calhoun County, was changed to Waterburgh on December 23, 1835, and later to Sheridan, a name the settlement took from the township when it was organized. The post office formerly called Bronson, in Kalamazoo County, had its name changed to Kalamazoo in 1836.

All of the name changes -- Bronson to Kalamazoo, Kalamazoo to Waterburgh, Kalamazoo to Newark and/or Saugatuck -- which occurred in two brief years led to much confusion. A Detroit newspaper which had apparently carried notice of the change from Kalamazoo to Saugatuck, further muddied the water by reporting in their August 24, 1836, issue: "We incorrectly stated some time since that the name of the Post Office known as Kalamazoo was changed to Saugatuck. The new name is *Waterburg*."

When the first post office was established at the Butler settlement on the banks of the Kalamazoo River on May 2, 1835, with Rensselaer R. Crosby as postmaster, the name given to that post office was **Saugatuck** (although in the early days it was sometimes spelled Saugatuc). Official post office records verify that there was never a post office at this site by any other name. The first post office was small and did not have a stamp, the postmaster providing the post mark and a note on the postage by hand. It also produced little revenue. In a letter dated December 28, 1835, Crosby wrote to his Congressional representative requesting that the Kalamazoo River be designated a port of entry and asking for an appointment as port collector. He carefully datelined his letter "Mouth Kalamazoo, Saugatuck P. O., Allegan Co., M. T." [Michigan Territory, although Michigan, by then, considered itself a state].

However, by 1838 Crosby was gone, and Oshea Wilder, who was a moving force in the settlement of **Singapore** near the mouth of the river, was complaining about the mail service. He asked Lucius Lyon, then a senator from Michigan, to establish a post office in his settlement. Wilder wrote, "You are personally acquainted with the, at present, isolated position of this place, & may imagine some of the difficulties & great inconveniences we Labour under for the want of a Post office and a proper transmission of the mail -- the office that has existed near Butlers is in a manner discontinued. The postmaster having moved to Illinois & every family residing in that place went with him or are going away in a few days -- the office papers were left with Butler -- & the place is so remote & difficult of access by us here that we might as well have no office, even if this should be continued. As it now is I find it safer to have our letters & papers addressed to Allegan about 28 miles inland & get them as we can as there is no regularity & only occasionally that a mail is sent from Allegan to this office (Saugatuck) & then by a raft going down the River -- "

An excerpt from official post office records showing the post office of Saugatuck established May 2, 1835.

Lyon replied that the post office at Saugatuck would probably be removed to Singapore as soon as a candidate for postmaster should be recommended of the "right politics." Andrew Jackson was in the White House and Democrats were hard to find in the woods of western Allegan County.

In April of 1838 Butler wrote Lyon with his side of the story. Butler wrote reasonably good English when he took the

35

time, but in this letter it would appear he was both in a hurry, and angry: "With much regret I take the liberty to trouble you to inform you of the situation of our Post office at this Place, but expect you have been advice of it by Mr. O. Wilder of Singapore some time sinse and perhaps by Messrs Hoffman or Beeson of Niles lately. Mr. Wilder read a parte of a Letter from a Friend of his from Washington in Decr. and I thought by the hand writing it was from you. he appeared verry angry said he intended publishing it, and it should cost the party 1000 votes at least, but I have not hurd of it being Published any more than reading it to others as he did to me. he wished me to consent to have the Office removed and tryed to bribe me. said he would not ask its removall without my consent but soon learned he had forward a Petition with many non residents names to it. when Mr. Crosby resigned he appointed me assist. last Augt. sins which I have wrote the Departement sevrl times informing them that there was not any Person to carry the mail and I had carried it mostly my selfe and sent it by private conveyance. and that I did not wish to act my selfe as P.M. but could no advices from them. I have not any objections to Singapore haveing an Office but know that this much the most Proper place if but one for it is the center of the Settlement. any assistance you could be to us would thankfully acknowledg and remembered by us proprietors and my self Individually."

In a post script he adds, "Propriators of this & Oxbow or Warehous fraction mouth of River which is expected to be connected by a Ship Canall 64 Rods, Hoffman & Beeson, Niles. Lt. James or J. H. Kinzie Chicago. J. R. Dorr Detroit. T. S. Morgan Oswego N. Y. J. Griffith W. H. Denning City N.Y."

The letter is datelined, "Kallamazoo" with an "Allegan C.H." [Court House] postal stamp on it. Not only does Butler, with some care, avoid mentioning the name of the post office which is the subject of the letter, he does not allude to "Newark" either. It is possible that if they had completed the canal to their warehouse near the lighthouse at the settlement that the 1844 map had called Kalamazoo, they would have given the entire operation the name Kalamazoo. However, even with poor mail service, they must have been aware that a much larger settlement in Kalamazoo County had acquired that name two years earlier.

From the list of proprietors, it is evident that Mason was no longer part of the project, his interest and perhaps additional shares had been purchased by Jacob Beeson of Niles, a merchant who also owned a warehouse and conducted a shipping business on the St. Joseph River. Beeson was a director of the Bank of Niles, a "wild cat" bank which would be destined to endure for less than three years, about the same life span as a similar bank in Singapore. Another new investor, T. S. Morgan of Oswego, New York, was related to the Morgan family of western New York State that also had invested considerable capital in Richmond, a settlement founded by John Allen several miles farther up the Kalamazoo River from the Butler enterprise. Josiah R. Dorr of Detroit, was a merchant and a partner with C. C. Trowbridge, a founder of Allegan, in the first sawmill built in Detroit. He was also a director of the Bank of St. Clair. W. H. Denning of New York was probably brought into the project by John Griffith, who maintained large business interests in New York City until after the economic crash of 1837.

Another new investor has a particularly interesting story. John Kinzie is often referred to as the father of Chicago. He worked most of his life in fur trading and other commerce with the Indians. About 1800 he first came to Chicago, but abandoned the town for several years following the massacre of 1812, although he and his family had been spared. The family returned to Chicago in 1816, and the elder Kinzie died in 1828, but his sons, James, by his first wife Margaret (McKenzie) Kinzie, and John Harris Kinzie, a child of his second wife, Eleanor (Little) Kinzie carried on the work. James lived in Chicago until 1836 when he moved to Wisconsin, first Racine, later Iowa County. John H. followed his father's work as a fur trader, and later was a protege of Michigan's Territorial

Governor Lewis Cass. He was appointed an Indian agent in Wisconsin in 1830, but resigned in 1833 and returned to Chicago to superintend the sale of lands and investments in the Chicago, Wisconsin, and Michigan area. It is unclear whether both were involved in the Saugatuck venture (or perhaps held the stock jointly, or with rights of survivorship) or whether Butler is uncertain of the first name of the Kinzie who held the interest.

The recipient of the letter, Senator Lucius Lyon, was well acquainted with the area and the settlements at both Singapore and Saugatuck. During his ten year career as a surveyor, 1823 to 1833, he had done most of the surveys in the eastern portion of Allegan County, and as a land speculator he held title to many acres of land in the Otsego and Trowbridge area as well as several small plots in Newark Township. In 1838, when a new lighthouse was being planned for the mouth of the Kalamazoo River, it was discovered that the owners of the land on which it was to be built were H. H. Comstock and Lucius Lyon.

There never was a post office established at Singapore, and Butler's appointment as Saugatuck postmaster, which was officially dated April 4, 1838, continued until Stephen A. Morrison took over January 18, 1842. Two things are evident in this heated, although slow-motion, exchange concerning the location of a post office to serve the area. The first is that Wilder was probably not a Democrat. The second, that William G. Butler did not especially like the name of Saugatuck.

The debate has raged for over a hundred years about whether the name Saugatuck was given to the area by local Indians or whether it was imported from Saugatuck, Connecticut, a small settlement on the Saugatuck River which is now within the corporate limits of the City of Westport.

Emerson Greenwood, Curator of the Great Lakes Division at the University of Michigan Museum of Anthro-

38

pology, when questioned prior to the centennial celebration of Saugatuck Village in 1968, wrote that it was a question difficult to answer as "the two tribes spoke the same language." However, in his more recent book, Vogel concluded that, "the name is not from the Potawatomi language, as some have indicated, but from the language of the Mohican of Connecticut or one of the small tribes related to them. The name is obviously a transfer from Saugatuck, Connecticut."

Saugatuck has been translated as "mouth of the river", or as Greenwood wrote more specifically as "a place on a lake near the mouth of a river." Both Saugatuck, Michigan, and Saugatuck, Connecticut, are so situated geographically.

In 1905 when Stephen A. Morrison died at the age of 84 his obituary in the *Commercial Record* offered an explanation:

MAN WHO NAMED VILLAGE
DIES OF OLD AGE.

Stephen A. Morrison was born in Barre, Vt., May 18, 1815, died of old age, in Saugatuck, May 4, 1905.

...with the exception of two years. When the first Post-Office was established, it was he who suggested that they call it "Saugatuck," an Indian word meaning "mouth of river."

Morrison, was from Vermont, but some sources claim he had spent a portion of his early life in Connecticut, not far from Saugatuck, on the Saugatuck River. It is, however, hard to understand how he could have named the post office which was begun in the spring of 1835, if he did not arrive in the area until 1837.

For more than 30 years the post office of Saugatuck existed within a growing town that was called by a number of titles depending on where you came from and what you were doing there. It was officially Kalamazoo, the name of the plat

39

and the name that should have been recorded on deeds and other papers concerning land. The name of Newark which had been taken by the township, seems to have been transferred informally to the village. The place was commonly referred to as **The Flats** because it was largely located on an expanse of flat land near the wide spot in the river.

In 1922 historian Henry Hudson Hutchins located a file of bills of lading kept by A. G. Spencer. These papers were dated 1856, 1857 and 1858. Hutchins wrote, "It is interesting to note that there was no special name for the place. Some bills are headed Kalamazoo, some Kalamazoo Harbor, while more are given at Newark. Business letters from nearby places were sent to Newark and Saugatuck. Nothing from away came to Saugatuck." He notes that one bill sent an order of bed frames from Kalamazoo (Kalamazoo County) to Kalamazoo (Allegan County).

A portion of the petition for incorporation showing the word "Saugatuck" which was pasted on top of "Belle Haven" on the paper.

When Saugatuck petitioned to be incorporated as a village in 1868 there was an effort to give it a different name.

On the document where the official wording states the name to be given to the new village, the words **Belle Haven** are written on the original petition, now found in county records. However, at some point in the proceedings, someone with a different handwriting than the person who had written out the bulk of the document wrote the name Saugatuck on a separate piece of paper and pasted it over the words Belle Haven, and the legislature officially incorporated the **Village of Saugatuck.**

In 1984 when the Village of Saugatuck voted to incorporate as a city, a great deal of discussion insued among the charter writers concerning the name. They wished to retain the Saugatuck part but considered using "City of Saugatuck Village" or "City of the Village of Saugatuck" as some communities have done to retain the flavor of the village in the official name. However, they opted instead, to become simply the **City of Saugatuck.**

Douglas

The south bank of the Kalamazoo River near Saugatuck was first cultivated in 1847 when Michael B. Spencer and Robert A. McDonald began farming operations on the high bank between the present sites of St. Peter's Catholic Church and Tara Restaurant (the first Tara was the old Spencer homestead). If they had a name for the settlement it has not been recorded. There is some evidence that both families actually lived on the Saugatuck side of the river, crossing by boat or bridge to tend their crops.

In 1851 Jonathan Wade, who had been involved with the mills in early Singapore, purchased land south of the river with a view toward building a saw mill. The first mill was constructed on a point of land which would now be just east of the highway bridge and was later described by an early settler as having "One muley saw, which is an upright arrangement and very slow and hard to operate, turning out but a few hundred feet of lumber in a day." An early reference to this small

41

settlement, including the mill and nearby residences, calls it **Millpoint**. This is a name which, in Michigan, is more commonly recognized as an early name of the community of Spring Lake, but it could have also been applied to the settlement south of Saugatuck. The geographical configurations are about the same.

In 1855 Wade decided to get out of the milling business and sold the north portion of his land to William F. Dutcher, who had arrived from Pennsylvania, via Chicago, with his large family. Dutcher added to the mill building and machinery and purchased additional land in section 16. The boundaries of his holdings were about the present day Center Street on the south, and Union Street on the west.

He had arrived with a family group of over ten members which included his wife, Lucinda (Dietrich) Dutcher, their oldest son, George Newburg Dutcher and his wife, Eliza; second son, Thomas Benton Dutcher (better known as Bent); a younger daughter, Elizabeth, who later became the wife of Lewis A. Upson; Frederic Henry May, the widower of their oldest daughter Mary Anne who had died in 1854 in Chicago; his son, William Augustus May; Frederic's mother, Mrs. Marianne May; Martin Dietrich, brother of Mrs. Dutcher, and his wife, and their twins, Emma and Emmett. It is not surprising that the settlement near the mill was called, at least informally, **Dutcherville**.

About 1860 William F. Dutcher decided to plat his land into village lots. He commissioned his son-in-law, Frederic H. May, to draw the map, and May accepted, according to an account later written by his son, William, "on the condition of being permitted to name the town." He named it **Douglas**, after his birthplace, Douglas, on the Isle of Man, a small semi-independent island in the Irish Sea with ties to Great Britain.

May is not an old-time Manx family name and how Frederic's parents landed on the tiny island involves a series of

42

circumstances in both hemispheres. Frederic's mother, Marianne, was born in 1796 on the island of Jamaica in the Caribbean. Her father was English by birth, but had immigrated to Jamaica where he had acquired a large holding of slaves and land. He died comparatively young in an accident, leaving a widow and four daughters. With no stern masculine hand at the helm their fortune and plantation rapidly declined and Marianne was sent back to England to go to school, and, perhaps, live with relatives.

At the age of 24 in Bristol on the west coast of England just south of Wales, she was married to Edmund May. The couple lived first on the island of Guernsey, one of the Channel Islands near the French coast, where the two oldest of their children were born, and afterwards moved to the Isle of Man in the Irish Sea. It was here that Frederic H. May was born in 1825. The city of Douglas is the capital of the Isle of Man and is named for the two rivers that unite within its boundaries the Dhoo River (from a Manx word meaning "dark") and the Glass River (a Manx word meaning "gray").

The May family moved to the United States in 1841, settling first in Brooklyn, New York, later moving to Pike County, Pennsylvania. The second year in Pennsylvania they amassed a supply of goods preparatory to opening a country store in Quicktown, three miles from the county seat of Milford, but lost both goods and residence in a fire. The family then moved to the mouth of the Lackawaxen River where Frederic was married to Mary Ann Dutcher.

The plat Frederic May drew of the planned Dutcher settlement, north of Center Street, was filed September 6, 1861. According to William May, "Before the plat of Douglas was drawn efforts were made to secure the co-operation of Mr. Wade who could thus make possible the creation of a larger town site, but he would have none of it." Jonathan Wade, who still owned the land to the south, had ideas of his own.

43

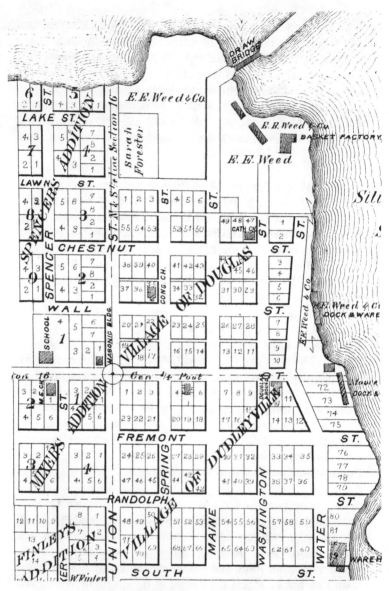

A 1913 map of the Village of Douglas showing the two plats which formed the incorporated village.

44

An undated and unsigned record in the Wade family has the other half of the story. "In 1860 Jonathan Wade wrote a letter to his brother, Dudley, then in Canada, that he was platting out a village here and was going to name it **Dudleyville**." Wade's plat was filed April 30, 1860. Shortly afterwards Dudley and his large family moved to Michigan. The northern boundary of Dudleyville (sometimes spelled Dudleysville) is Center Street.

For ten years there existed, along the south bank of the Kalamazoo, two rival towns, separated by a single street -- Douglas to the north, Dudleyville to the south. Especially after the departure of Dudley, however, the name of Douglas seemed to be the more generally accepted one. The post office, established in 1866 by Dyer C. Putnam (on the Dudleyville side of Center Street), was called Douglas. In the Saugatuck newspaper, which began publication in 1868, the settlement across the river was always referred to as Douglas.

In the decade that elapsed between the drawing of the two plats and the incorporation of the Village of Douglas in 1870, nearly all of the Wades and most of the Dutchers left the area. Some members of both families migrated north to the area around Cadillac where the Dutcher men started a wood products business known as the Douglas Manufacturing Co. There is still a small body of water in the Cadillac area known as Dutcher Pond. Several of the Dutcher men either remained in Allegan County or returned from Cadillac and started a mill and coal yard in Fennville where they experienced their most prosperous times, milling lumber for the rebuilding of Fennville, Holland and Chicago following the disastrous fires of 1871. Frederic May worked across the country building railroads and telegraph lines. At some point he moved to Allegan, and later to New Jersey where he was the head of the American Rapid Telegraph Company prior to his death in 1908.

Frank Wade, who had been the first white child born in the settlement, January 9, 1853, lived in Douglas virtually all his life. He was village president for five years and on the village council for 21 years. After his marriage to Nettie Hutchinson he lived in a small house two doors east of the Congregational Church on Wall Street, on the Douglas side of town. It was Frank, in later years, who reported that as a boy he had attended a meeting where the town was named after Stephen A. Douglas, the 1860 Democratic candidate for president who had lost out to Abraham Lincoln.

A Chicago newspaper in 1871 ran an article on resort areas of Western Michigan and the description of Saugatuck mentioned Douglas ". . . across Lake Kalamazoo to the southward is the twin brother of Saugatuck, and its friendly rival. bearing the name of Douglas, in honor of the deceased statesman."

William A. May responded, "I find you are puzzled as to the origin of the name 'Douglas.' Being conversant with the christening of said village, I would like to say that the village of Douglas was platted by my grandfather, William F. Dutcher, and named after Douglas, capital of the Isle of Man, and birthplace of my father, Frederic H. May, now of Allegan; in fact my father named the place. The general impression that the name was after Senator Stephen Douglass is wrong . . . The Dutcher men were all Democrats in politics, and in the campaign of 1860 being supporters of Stephen A. Douglas, the Democratic nominee for president, many people got the idea that the town had been named in honor of Mr. Douglas, but that is not true, for Mr. May was in politics, a rabid Republican, and having the right to name the town would never have consented to call it after the Democratic nominee. Party feeling ran too high in those days for such a thing to be possible."

The conclusion, drawn with the advantage of historical perspective, is that the various residents of the town accepted the name Douglas for a variety of reasons, although its origin is clearly linked to the birthplace of Frederic May on the Isle of Man.

A SONG OF SAUGATUCK

By Howard L. Smith

(Read at the annual banquet to the Fursman Art Class at Riverside Hotel.)

I sing the sand of Saugatuck,
That water never turns to muck;
I sing the placid Kalamazoo,
And the gay and festive artist crew
Who all around their paint rags threw;
I sing the skies of turquoise blue,
The bathing suits of every hue --
And all that they present to view.

I sing the shores of Saugatuck
(I sing much like a Mallard duck) --
The waves that take such liberty
With nymphs who sport decollete;
I sing the pictures that we painted,
At sight of which no one has fainted;
I sing of pancakes and of bacon,
Which ere I came had all been taken.

If I had Zaidee's voice and pluck
I'd sing the woods of Saugatuck,
And make you think the nightingale
Was but a poor and piping quail.
I'd sing the beech tree's boll unshaven,
Upon whose bark I find engraven
The names of lovers -- a score or so --
Each soon will have another beau.

I'd sing the deep wood's grateful shade,
The cedared aisles, the ferny glade;
The hemlock's feathery, swaying form;
The oak that battles with the storm.'
But these, alas, are not for me,
Whose song must strike some lower key
More suited to a muse that's rusty
And to a land that's hot and dusty.

I've known of men who've traveled much,
Who've seen the Romans and the Dutch.
Who know the Chinese and the Japs,
And even ventured 'mongst the Lapps,
Who've crossed the Andes and the Rhine,
And seen the midnight sun to shine.
But he is surely out of luck
Who never, never Saugatuck.

(The Fursman Art Class was part of what was sometimes called the Ox-Bow Summer School of Painting which met in the Riverside Hotel and adjoining buildings on the old ox-bow of the river directly west of Saugatuck, between the village and Lake Michigan. At the end of each summer season there is a banquet closing the year's activity and providing a burial for times past. The landscape of the school grounds is dotted with artistically designed "tombstones" for years past, and the annual event is still a much hallowed tradition at the school, now called the Ox-Bow Summer School of Art and administered in association with the Chicago Art Institute. This whimsical, but cleverly designed, poetic offering was part of the celebration in 1919.)

The Wreck of the Hippocampus

The atmosphere in the twin towns of St. Joseph and Benton Harbor was glum September 11, 1868. The steamer *Hippocampus*, which had only that spring established a regular route between the St. Joseph River and Chicago, was missing. The boat had left on Monday, September 7, laden with baskets of peaches and a human cargo of more than 30 (passengers and crew) and had not been heard from since.

The first night, when the *Hippocampus* did not arrive in Chicago, the people blamed the delay on a dense fog which had blanketed lower Lake Michigan. The hope was that, when visibility improved, the boat would be found, perhaps having experienced mechanical difficulties. Even on Wednesday some still hoped that survivors might yet be found in the mild waters of early September clinging to floating debris.

But the week wore on. When the vessel had been missing five days the town began to accept its loss. Most distraught of all was the ship's usual captain and part-owner, John Morrison. He had been ill, largely from overwork, at the time of the ship's departure and had persuaded his friend, Captain Henry Brown, to take the trip. Not only did Captain Morrison feel in some way responsible for the loss, but there was the personal grief of losing his 18-year-old son, Charles, who had shipped as wheelsman.

As the townspeople went numbly about their work they heard whistles and bells from the mouth of the river. The sound grew louder as more boats joined in. Those near the river bank looked in amazement as the *W. B. Minter*, a tug from Saugatuck, about 40 miles north of St. Joseph on the eastern shore of Lake Michigan, steamed up the river, her whistle sounding, and 15 of the passengers and crew of the ill-fated *Hippocampus* waving happily from her deck, apparently well-fed and healthy, and all outfitted in brand new suits.

The tug W. B. Minter

The September 12, 1868, edition of the *Saugatuck Commercial* gives a modest account of the incident:

STEAMBOAT DISASTER

All speculation as to the fate of the Propeller Hippocampus has been set at rest by the arrival of the survivors, fifteen in all, they having been picked up by the Scow Trio, Johnson, Master, arriving here Friday morning quite early.

The Disaster is now known to be caused as it was supposed by overloading. Capt. Brown states that she gave a lurch and a heavy sea striking her at the same time tore off her entire upper works, the hull sinking at once. The survivors clung to the floating pieces of the cabin and wheel-house and after being beaten about by the wind and waves for two days and nights, were at last recovered by Capt. Johnson of the Scow Trio, who did all in his power to relieve the wants and sufferings of the survivors.

They were kindly cared for here and the Tug "W. B. Minter" took them to St. Joseph as soon as possible after their arrival.

The following is a list of the passengers and crew, lost and saved;

CREW SAVED. -- H. B. Brown Master, J. P. Bloom Clerk, Chas. Morrison Wheelsman, Chas. Russel, Cyrus Rittenhouse, colored, T. C. Johnson, colored, M. Robinson, A. Howard and T. E. Hopper.

PASSENGERS SAVED. -- B. Baley, C. N. Hatch, James Trumble, George A. Fuller, J. Riford and Joseph Cooley.

CREW LOST. -- R. Ritchardson, Mate, R. Eustell, Engineer, William Brown, Engineer, Daniel Moore, Cook, Chas. Williams, colored, David Taylor, colored, J. Wright, colored, H. Manuel, colored, G. B. Van Horn colored, Warren Brant, A. Woodden, E. VanNorten, M. Bake, D. James and F. Mathews.

PASSENGERS LOST. -- Uisal Higbey, A. Burridge, J. K. Burridge, W. S. Watson, Alva Palmer, J. Whitney, Wm. Vaughan, J. Shrum, R. K. Burk, and J. Marpel.

(Many of the names on this list of those lost do not match up with a similar list in the St. Joseph paper in spelling or initials, but this is the way the Saugatuck paper recorded it.) The following week, in the issue of September 26, 1868, the *Commercial* carried a full account of the disaster, sent from St. Joseph by Captain Brown.

FURTHER FROM THE HIPPOCAMPUS
Statement of Captain Brown

I was in command of the steamer Hippocampus Monday night last. She left St. Joseph at 11 in the evening. Had on board 7001 packages of peaches. The sea commenced rolling from the southward. The wind commenced increasing from the time we left here. The vessel commenced to roll badly about 1 o'clock, but nothing extraordinary occurred until about half past 2. At this time I went into the engine room and the fire hold to see if there was any water in her but found none. I then went with the wheels-man, Charles Morrison, down forward, below decks into the forepeak, to see if there was any water down there but found none. Came on deck and found she was making still heavier rolls, the wind increasing. I remarked to the wheelsman, "We must lighten her of her cargo." Coming on deck I told the wheelsman to summon the crew and throw the peaches from the promenade deck. I did this in a loud tone of voice. This command was heard by the passengers who then rushed on deck in great confusion. The steamer was now settling rapidly and before any freight could be thrown overboard the water commenced pouring into the engine room and into the hold; at the same time the vessel went over on her port side and went down in two minutes.

The passengers had retired but sprang from their berths and ran out on the weather side of the cabin, on hearing my command to throw the freight overboard. Much confusion ensued. I cried out, "Clear away the life-boat." There were no peaches in the life boat. At this time I was in the pilot house, and ordered the helm hard a-port, which was executed. Being convinced she was going over and seeing nothing further could be done I came from the pilot house and started forward to get hold of the hatch, but the boat had careened so far that I slid into the water and caught hold of the rigging of the mast and floated along retaining my hold until I reached the cross trees of the mast. To prevent being entangled in the gear, and to avoid the suction of the sinking vessel I swam to the floating desk and tried to buoy myself up with that. I was soon hailed by the wheelshand Morrison. I went to him and got on his raft, consisting of one side of the cabin. Passengers and crew all around in *debris*, all crying for help, and calling to a passing schooner -- I think the Humbolt -- which was perhaps half a mile away.

Shortly after getting on the raft I found another raft on which was Captain Trimble, J. Riford, Hatch and others. We remained near each other till daylight at which time we picked up Fuller. We held the two rafts together by means of a pole. About two hours before daylight we thought best to fasten the two rafts together. About this time we found Bloom and Johnson on another raft. We held to them by a pole, thus keeping together for about an hour. The sea rising we thought best to separate the rafts for fear of coming together and breaking up. We drifted apart, our raft going faster than Bloom's. The sea dashed over us up to our waists all day. About 10 o'clock in the forenoon we sighted a vessel about four miles to our lee. We signaled but to no purpose. At 2 or 3 o'clock in the afternoon we were about a mile from Bloom and Johnson. They paddled to us and we joined our rafts together, and all remained together till next morning when we saw a vessel light. We hailed her with all our might but failed to make them hear us. We gave up all hopes of rescue from that vessel. Shortly after this we discovered another light which we hailed. We thought she heard us and felt encouraged. This was about 4 o'clock Wednesday morning. We continued hallooing until we were heard and the vessel, the scow Trio, Captain Johnson, bound from Chicago to Saugatuck, came to our rescue. We learned they had picked up Robinson and left on Robinson's raft a dead boy who is not known. They left the boy because hearing our cries they desired to hasten to our rescue.

The Trio now cruised about in hopes of finding others. In about an hour we found the lifeboat bottom side up which was taken on board. We just then discovered another object half a mile away, this proved to be a section of the pilot house, on which was lashed Bailey. We lowered a boat and took him on board. We continued to cruise about, perhaps an hour longer and then went on our way to Saugatuck.

It is not recorded precisely where the wreck occurred, or where the survivors were picked up. The scow *Trio* was built near Pier Cove, Ganges Township, Allegan County in 1864 by Joseph St. Germain, who was living in Singapore as early as 1845. St. Germain had began his work in the boatbuilding trade as a caulker. The first owners of record were Captain Charles M. Link of Ganges, Benjamin B. Tourtellotte of Glenn and Willard S. Priest with Link serving as the first master. The ship's home base was Pier Cove, a shallow indentation along the coast about eight miles south of Saugatuck where a pier was built out into the lake in 1849 to ship cordwood and tanbark.

The *Trio* was a schooner-scow of 90 gross tons capacity (66 net tons) and was 75.3 feet long with an 18.3 foot beam. The schooner-scow was a craft peculiar to the Great Lakes. A fully rigged sailing ship, the hull of a schooner-scow had straight sides, usually squared ends, and relatively shallow draft. "Deck over an outsized cement mason's mud box, add a jibboom, a few masts, deckhouse and rudder . . . the result will be close to the appearance of the average schooner-scow," one contemporary writer explained. The ships were often used when there was a need to negotiate shallow water; the *Trio* drew but six feet four inches of water, where an average keeled sailing ship would require ten or more. An added advantage of the schooner-scow was that it cost less and required less skill to build than the conventional sailing craft. However, even with a portable centerboard, a scow did not handle quite as well in a heavy sea. One account of the rescue of the *Hippocampus* survivors indicates that after she picked up the men from their makeshift rafts the *Trio*, now overloaded herself, had to lay to in the low swell waiting for a satisfactory wind to sail to Saugatuck.

The Trio (at left) docked in Milwaukee harbor in the 1880s.

When they arrived in Saugatuck the survivors were taken to various homes and given an opportunity to bathe and take a hot meal, for they had not eaten in 38 hours. In 1868 there were two mills still functioning at Singapore, near the mouth of the river, and several in the settlement of Saugatuck. At least two of these mills were owned by O. R. Johnson and Co. which also ran a large general store in a building that still stands on Water Street in Saugatuck. Francis B. Stockbridge (later a U. S. Senator from Kalamazoo) was manager of the Saugatuck store and a partner with Johnson in several other business enterprises. Apparently at his own expense he provided each of the survivors with a new suit of clothing, replacing their watersoaked, tattered garments.

There was no telegraph connection between the towns along Lake Michigan in 1868 and no way of sending a message to relatives and friends in St. Joseph. After the survivors had eaten and been re-outfitted they were given places in Saugatuck homes for the night. Early the next morning, the cost apparently underwritten by Stockbridge and tug owner Captain W. B. Minter, the *Minter* was fired up and the rescued were on their way home.

It was generally conceded that the immense load of peaches (some sources say 7000, others more than 8000 baskets) was the primary cause of the foundering. Peaches were a perishable cargo and, if they did not make the next boat, all profit was generally lost. Since fruit had to be moved by hand, a basket at a time, there was a tendency to leave the load on deck rather than moving it to a below-decks cargo area. Shippers also liked the on-deck position for the natural refrigeration provided by the night breeze. The captain's statement that "there were no peaches in the lifeboat" would tend to confirm the rumors that lifeboats on deck often served as handy receptacles for fruit baskets.

An additional problem was noted by wheelsman Charles Morrison, who later gave an account that it was his feeling that the boat, riding low in the water because of the large cargo, struck something as it rounded the point near the wing dam leaving port at St. Joseph. The impact opened a seam which widened in the rough sea. Morrison said he had tried to

56

sleep but was uneasy because the ship was acting strange. He got up from his bunk and asked the wheelsman on duty whether he noticed anything out of the ordinary, and the man said that the vessel was "steering hard." He and Captain Brown took a lantern and inspected the hold. They found no water due to two watertight bulkheads, but he heard water in the bilges.

Joseph Riford of Benton Harbor, one of the survivors, floundered about in the water after the ship went down until he found a floating chair. Using it to buoy himself, he joined the others on the makeshift raft. He was asked to pray, and Cy Rittenhouse, one of the survivors, said later he had never heard anyone pray so earnestly or devoutly. "He prayed in all sincerity, not because he was scared and not for himself, but for all on the wave-washed raft."

Another survivor Edward N. Hatch wrote later, "The sea was running high . . . there was thunder and lightning during the day and it rained hard. We felt gloomy and discouraged. Mr. Riford, an old gentlemen of Benton Harbor, cheered us and, at the request of Captain Brown, prayed for our deliverance. While praying all sat quiet as possible. After the prayer all promised to be better men and Christians if they reached shore. We were exhorted to this by Riford." Shortly after the prayer was finished the *Trio* arrived.

At the time of the rescue the *Trio* was under the command of Captain Alexander A. Johnson, an old saltwater sailor who had come to Allegan County in 1849 to take command of the *Octavia*, a lumber schooner built at Singapore. It turned out that lumber was not in sufficient demand at that time to support a full-time boat and the schooner was sold to Chicago interests in 1852. About this time Captain Johnson married and retired to a farm in Ganges Township.

The pier at Pier Cove was one of many built in that era along the eastern shore of Lake Michigan. They were busy ports during the cordwood and tanbark days and then fell into disuse, only to be revived in the 1880s when fruit shipping made them again profitable. In about 1885 one of the *Trio's* builders, Captain Link, became part owner of a second pier at Pier Cove. There was a similar pier built in 1860 at Glenn, three and a half miles south of Pier Cove, and D. D. Tourtellotte was later an officer in the Glenn Pier Company. Between Pier Cove and Glenn, from 1854 to about 1875, there was another pier at Plummerville which serviced a local tanning industry, and later was used by area fruit growers.

The *Hippocampus* was built by George Hanson and launched in the summer of 1866 at St. Joseph. Originally Captain Morrison, Curtis W. Boughton and John C. Shaw, all of the St. Joseph area, owned equal shares in the venture, but in the enrollment dated March 23, 1868, Shaw had apparently provided additional capital and owned 96 shares, or 65 percent of the investment. Boughton's share was down to about 11 percent, and John Morrison owned only 24 percent, although he is still listed as managing owner.

"Hippocampus" is the Latin name for a sea horse. She was approximately 82 feet in length with an 18 foot beam and a depth of seven feet. She was certified for 152.91 gross tons. The ship had only that March begun regular trips between St. Joseph and Chicago. An ad in the March 21, 1868, *Saint Joseph Saturday Herald* stated:

PROPELLER HIPPOCAMPUS

This new and staunch vessel, with Captain John Morrison in command, is now making regular trips between this port and Chicago. Passenger fare $1.00; fare back, $1.00. Freight rates as low as possible.
Boughton & Morrison, agents, Saint Joseph.

The *William B. Minter*, 25.61 gross tons, had been launched in June of 1868 at Saugatuck. She was constructed by master builder James W. McMillan and was 53 feet long with a 15 foot beam. In 1868 her owners of record were Captain William B. Minter and Harlow Joslyn, both of Saugatuck, and her enrolled captain was Amariah H. Coates, commonly called "Ami," one of six Coates brothers who piloted boats from Saugatuck for more than 40 years. The *Minter* and the propeller *Ira Chaffee*, which had begun regular trips to Chicago that summer, were among the first steam-powered vessels built on the Kalamazoo River. The *Minter* was purchased the following year by Otis R. Johnson, Francis B. Stockbridge, Lintsford B. Coates and A. H. Coates, all actively engaged in lumbering at Saugatuck and Singapore. She was later owned by the Saugatuck Lumber Co., and, in 1876, became the property of the Mackinaw Lumber Co., another sawmill venture begun by the same men near St. Ignace. On June 6, 1883, the lumber company surrendered the enrollment, noting that the boat was "out of commission." She was later purchased by John C. Gram of Au Sable and may have been used in his wrecking and dredging business until the final surrender of her papers November 26, 1901 at Port Huron where it was noted that the vessel was "abandoned as unfit for service lying at or near Manistique."

The Case of the Yellow Dog

Although it was a white dog that was so highly prized by the early Indians for ritual sacrifice on Mount Baldhead, it was a yellow dog that made the news in 1898.

In early summer there had been a number of complaints about dogs running loose in the Village of Saugatuck, and a report of at least one individual who had been bitten by a stray dog. There was already a law on the books that required the muzzling of dogs within the village limits in the summer, but it was universally ignored. At the July meeting of the Saugatuck Village Council the problem was discussed and the *Lakeshore Commercial* reported in the July 8 issue:

"The village officers have received orders to enforce the dog muzzling law and are expected to shoot every unmuzzled dog found running at large during the next two months."

The following week the editor gave an added nudge to the village marshal with a paragraph which noted, "The resolution of the council to enforce the dog ordinance has resulted in the muzzling of about two per cent of the canines of the place. So long as the council allows its orders to be thus treated with contempt, none of its acts will receive much respect."

The challenge was clearly in the council's court and the marshal on the prowl. Finally, he located an unmuzzled dog and instead of shooting it issued a summons. According to the August 5, 1898, *Lakeshore Commercial*:

"D. L. Barber is the first victim of the dog crusade, having been brought to book for not muzzling his dog. The trial is set for next Monday, when Charles Thew, as village attorney will appear for the people. Mr. Barber disavows the ownership of the dog, and swears in several languages that his defense will stop nothing short of the supreme court."

Daniel L. Barber, the defendant in this case, was one of the village's most stalwart citizens. He had been in the area since about 1858, working fourteen years for Johnson and Stockbridge in Singapore, and in their Saugatuck store. In 1873 he invested in a dry goods store in partnership with A. B. Taylor. The partnership was dissolved in 1879, and both men opened their own stores in Saugatuck. Barber was a longtime member of the Saugatuck School Board and served as president of the village 1875-76, and again in 1883.

Along with the notice of the trial, the Saugatuck paper carried the following newsy rhyme:

> Barber had a yellow dog
> But wouldn't buy a muzzle;
> The marshal saw his duty clear
> And proved the law no puzzle.
> He took his neighbor up to court
> With much indignant outburst.
> But Barber swore he'd pay no fine --
> He'd see 'em all in h--l first.
> And now the lawyers, like the dog,
> With free unmuzzled jaw,
> Will howl and yelp in an attempt
> To vindicate the law.

For some reason, unstated in the newspapers, the court trial was postponed, and the August 12 newspaper noted: "The famous 'yellow dog case' will occupy the attention of Justice Leland next Saturday morning. If the performers are feeling well there will be a good show."

The following week, while out-of-town readers rushed to their *Lakeshore Commercial* hoping for a thorough and probably humorous account of the trial, there was only this brief paragraph:

> The case against D. L. Barber for failure to muzzle his dog was dismissed when it came up before Justice Leland last Saturday morning. Mr. Barber convinced the court that he was not the owner of the "yellow dog."

Barber continued to operate a general store in Saugatuck taking into partnership his daughter Caddie and her husband, Will J. Hancock. Although Hancock was a great-great grandson of John Hancock, one of the signers of the Declaration of Independence, his biggest claim to fame in Saugatuck was his narrow escape from losing his life when the steamship *Chicora* went down in 1895. He had worked many years for Graham and Morton and was the regular purser of the steamship. However, he had missed several trips in the winter of 1895 to be with his wife who was seriously ill. The company tried to send him a telegram recalling him to duty before the ship left port on her last trip, but the message had not reached him in time to take the train to Milwaukee. The *Chicora* disappeared, with all hands, probably somewhere near the eastern shore of Lake Michigan, January 21, 1895, and Hancock led the search for survivors and later coordinated unsuccessful efforts to locate the sunken hulk. He was later assigned to other Graham and Morton ships, including the *City of Milwaukee* and the *City of Chicago*. When he was not out on the lakes, he worked in the Saugatuck store with his wife and father-in-law until the building burned to the ground in 1904. Plans to rebuild in the spring were canceled after the death of Caddie (Barber) Hancock during the winter, and Barber retired to his fruit farm east of Saugatuck. He died in 1909.

No one has recorded what happened to the yellow dog.

A Twentieth Century Steamboat

From the days of the early native Americans who turned out birchbark canoes and dugout vessels along the banks of the Kalamazoo, shipbuilding has been an important industry. More than 200 commercial ships were built in Saugatuck and uncounted hundreds of small yachts, sailboats, and rowing craft.

Beginning in the 1830s and continuing to about the turn of the century Saugatuck shipyards were bustling. Lumber suitable for ship construction was available locally, a large skilled labor force lived in the community, and Saugatuck steamers and tugs were in demand in Chicago, Milwaukee, Green Bay, and other important Great Lakes' ports. But by 1900 the industry was winding down. Continued problems with shoaling at the mouth of the river limited the boatbuilders to vessels of shallow draft, railroads had taken over much of the freight and passenger traffic, and the wooden ships that Saugatuck built so well were replaced by steel-hulled models.

However, some were not ready to give up so easily. Although there had been no commercial vessel of consequence built along the banks of the Kalamazoo since 1898, Captain William P. Wilson laid the keel for a new steamer in December of 1911. He had been trying to purchase a boat for several years but had been unable to find a suitable vessel. Wilson already owned one boat, the small steamship *John A. Aliber* which he and George Harvey had built in the winter of 1897, but he needed a second boat, larger than the *Aliber* and suitable for both the fruit trade and passenger excursions.

William P. Wilson was the son of Thomas Wilson, a native of England and originally a brickmaker, who had come to America in 1848 and obtained a position as a steamboat engineer on the Mississippi River. About 1850 Thomas moved to Singapore at the mouth of the Kalamazoo River where he served as engineer at one of the sawmills. It was here that his son, William, was born in 1861. William's mother, who was to lend her name to his new steamboat, was Anna Cuthbert (Abbey) Wilson, a native of County Carlow, Ireland. William followed his father into the engineer's trade. He began seasonal work on boats as a young man and served as second engineer of the *A. B. Taylor*, owned by Rogers and Bird, as early as 1888. Then, in 1897, he became master of the *Aliber*.

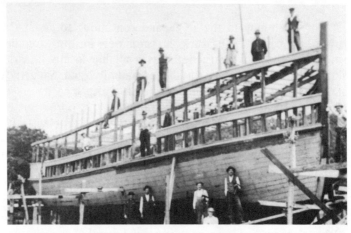

The Anna C. Wilson under construction in the spring of 1912.

After an unusually late-in-the-season start, work was rushed to try to get the vessel ready for the summer season and in the June 21, 1912, edition of the *Commercial-Record*, the boat's beginning was described under the headline "The Anna C. Wilson is Launched."

> The ceremonies appropriate to the launching of a ship were carried out on the Wilson dock Saturday afternoon when the boat which Capt. W. P. Wilson and Henry Randall have been building the past winter, was christened.
> A large crowd was present from Ganges, Chicago and other places besides Saugatuck

and Douglas when Rev. L. A. Lash made a few remarks before the tug Walter S. took the line to pull the craft into the water. She was started twice, the second time just as she was about to go into the river. Miss Mary Randall broke the bottle and proclaimed her the Anna C. Wilson, in honor of Capt. Wilson's mother of Ganges who was present at the ceremony and as much surprised by learning the name as anyone.

It was unfortunate that the tug pulled a little up stream and the ways slid sideways so the craft fell over partly on her side, which made it necessary to have her raised before she could finally be launched. The job was finished Tuesday about noon.

The Anna C. Wilson is an exceptionally well built boat and would be ready to make her maiden trip by July 1st if the boiler could be here by that time, but it is not expected so soon. She is 105 feet long [According to her official papers she was 91 feet long] by 20 feet and 4 inches beam. She has a new 16x16 Port Huron engine and her boiler will be 10x6 1/2 capable of carrying 140 pounds of steam. Her capacity is about 100 tons or three times the capacity of the Aliber. She is made of the best of material, as is proven by the fact that all the trouble in getting her into the water did not loosen the seams.

She will take the place of the Aliber on the Saugatuck and South Haven run, and Capt. Wilson tells us that with her equipment of machinery she will be able to make 12 miles an hour.

Pictures reveal that the upperworks were only roughed in at the time of launching. The task of finishing the carpentry and final outfitting must have taken longer than expected, because it was not until the August 23 issue of the newspaper that the *Wilson* was reported ready for business:

The launch of the Anna C. Wilson

"The Anna C. Wilson made her maiden trip Saturday afternoon to South Haven. Everything went well and, although no attempt was made to break any time records, she made about twelve miles an hour. Capt. Wilson tells us this will be about the speed she will be run at most of the time. She is now making regular trips in place of the Aliber, which boat had an accident last week. When only a short way out of South Haven, she blew out her cylinder head and three gasoline boats towed her back into port. A tug brought her up here, and if she can be repaired in time she will take up her regular run and the Anna C. Wilson will carry excursions."

In the same paper was the notice: "The steamer Anna C. Wilson will make an excursion to South Haven Saturday, Aug. 24, leaving the skating rink dock at 10:30 A.M. and returning at 5:30 P.M."

However, bad luck continued to dog the vessel and the August 30 paper reported: "On account of bad weather the Anna C. Wilson did not make the excursion to South Haven Saturday but will make the trip tomorrow. Yesterday she took an excursion to Macatawa." Although the weather remained cool, the following week it was reported: "About fifty in all went on the excursion on the Anna C. Wilson to South Haven Saturday."

In the fall of her maiden year the dock property was improved, but it was not until the middle of December that the Wilson was ready for the seasonal hiatus: "The Str. Aliber has been laid up for the season, but the Wilson will bring a load of coal from Holland before ending her season. Capt. Wilson is now at work building a new dock. Piles are being driven in a northeasterly direction starting at the warehouse and extending out into the water at an angle of about 30 degrees. This will allow boats to make a better landing in all kinds of weather. A new and much larger warehouse will replace the old one and the dock property will be improved in other ways." The Wilson boat dock was located at the north end of Butler Street, just north of what was later known as Willow Park. After the Crawford Transportation Co. ceased business in 1912, Wilson also bought the old Crawford pier, sometimes called the Eastland dock or the Red Dock, on the Douglas side of the river, about where the *Keewatin* later was permanently berthed.

The engine in the *Wilson* was replaced in 1915 with a two-cylinder fore and aft steam engine from the Montague Iron Works with 12- and 24-inch cylinders and a 20-inch stroke, producing 150 horsepower. The following year more staterooms were added, creating sleeping accommodations for 16 passengers, probably the height of her space as an overnight boat.

Although both the *Aliber* and the *Wilson* occasionally went all the way into Chicago, their most common route, especially in later years, was to make connections with larger boats that went into the big city. Together, the two boats were known as the East Shore Line. Commonly the *Wilson* went south, stopping at Pier Cove and the Glenn pier and making connections with the Dunkley-Williams Line out of South Haven, and thé *Aliber* went north connecting with Graham and Morton, and other boatlines, in Holland, but routes changed frequently.

For a number of years the *Wilson* ran a seasonal pattern, carrying freight from South Haven to Chicago early in the season until traffic increased to the point that a larger boat was needed. She then ran from Saugatuck to South Haven, or, when bigger boats muscled into the Saugatuck market, from the piers to South Haven. Captain Wilson bought one of the piers at Pier Cove and had control over its fruit trade, but his boats also carried other freight. In 1917 the *Wilson* was equipped with an elevator to facilitate loading pianos that were built in South Haven and shipped south. In addition, she took occasional excursions and, after the main season, operated well into the winter carrying freight on contract.

The *Anna C. Wilson* was sold in 1920 to Howard C. Morgan of Traverse City for approximately $20,000. She would be chartered to come south and take the South Haven-Chicago run until the larger boats were needed in the spring, then return to Traverse City carrying cider apples from various Lake Michigan ports to the Morgan company's cider mill and canning factory. Later the *Wilson* would take the finished products to market. She was also called to fill in for the *Aliber* on the Saugatuck-Holland run in October of 1922 when the *Aliber* sank in Macatawa Lake following an encounter with the Holland pier in a rough sea.

Captain William P. Wilson retired to his home by the river in Saugatuck when the boat was sold in 1920. He died in 1940. After the retirement of his father, Captain Frank E. Wilson, took over as master of the *Wilson*, sailing it for the Morgan Company, until the summer of 1922 when he died unexpectedly after a brief illness.

The Anna C. Wilson, in this photograph taken about 1915, is tied up alongside the East Shore Pavilion, where Wicks Parks was later located. In the foreground is the chain ferry scow crossing the river with the small rowboat, used when there were only one or two passengers, in tow.

69

By 1923 she was replaced in Traverse City and began sailing between Chicago and Michigan City during the week and making weekend excursion between Jackson Park and Navy Pier along the Chicago lakefront. For the latter run the upper deck was opened up and the ship reduced to 83 gross tons.

Despite her near disastrous launching and many small problems during her first year in business the *Wilson* had a relatively uneventful career. Her narrowest escape occurred in April of 1916, when she was caught in a severe storm on the way to Chicago and two of her life boats were swept away. One was found at South Chicago and the other at Indiana Harbor. The equipment was lost, but the hulls were returned.

A small ship but a "pretty little model" according to a steamship man who knew her, the boat was much admired. In 1924 Capt. W. P. Wilson was surprised to receive a letter, written in Spanish, from the owner of a steamship line in Barranquilla, Columbia, South America, who had seen a picture of the *Wilson* and asked the captain to build him a similar vessel. Wilson was flattered but declined to get back into the steamboat-building business.

By 1928 the *Anna C. Wilson* was owned by the Western Transportation Company of Chicago. In 1931 she was acquired by Edward C. Hintze of Michigan City, who ran her between Navy Pier and Jackson Park for the West Ports Steamboat Company. Hintze was owner of record when she was taken to at Michigan City about 1934. A 1941 photograph shows her still more-or-less afloat, tied to the bank at the water's edge, with jagged holes where three forward portholes had been hacked from the hull. She was officially listed as abandoned in 1943. As water levels changed, she grounded in the mud of the river bank, and was stripped of most burnable wood. For years Saugatuck travelers to Chicago would pass over the U. S. 12 bridge at Michigan City and look down at the riverbank where she lay, machinery and upperworks missing, a pigeon roost with many a nautical tale to tell.

A Sunken Sawlog, Conflicting
Claims and a Lawsuit

The sawlog is the property of Captain Brittain.

Captain Wilson may collect pay for salvage, storage, etc.

So a jury decided in Justice Simonson's court Saturday after hearing the evidence and the oratory of Lawyer Hoffman for Brittain and Lawyer Gardner for Wilson.

So when Captain Brittain pays the storage bill he may have the log sawed up into rather high priced lumber.

The innocent log, forgotten and unmourned, for years had rested in quiet oblivion and the equally quiet mud on the bottom of the Kalamazoo River until resurrected in the dredging operations last summer.

The dredgers had no use for a log so they turned it over to Captain Wilson, on condition that he get it ashore and keep it there.

Captain Brittain sauntering jauntily by caught the trend and at once set up the claim that the log was a maverick escaped years ago from the Brittain ship yard.

Followed months of jockeying for tactical advantage by the captains two. Then the lawsuit and the decision.

Puck said it.

-- *Commercial Record*
March 30, 1923

[What Puck said, in Shakespeare's *A Midsummer Night's Dream,* is "Lord, what fools these mortals be!"]

The Day the Pavilion Burned

When the Big Pavilion of Saugatuck was built in 1909, it was billed as "the brightest spot on the Great Lakes." Old residents will tell you it was a dance hall unparalleled -- an enchanted place.

As originally constructed the large, red-painted, round-roofed building contained a 110 by 60 foot dance floor, with a 25 foot promenade and various refreshment concessions around the edge. There was also an outdoor movie theater, and, if you came early enough in the evening, for one admission you could see the movie before joining the dancing crowd in the big ballroom. Proper decorum was demanded, and two masters of ceremony circulated to make sure that all dancers were properly attired. Men's suit coats and collars were to be buttoned at all times. Women's dresses covered the ankles and hat pins were forbidden.

In 1909 electricity had not yet come to Saugatuck, but the new dance hall had its own dynamo to power the thousands of colored lights that outlined the curved roof and towers outside and lined the arches in the ballroom. They were controlled by a series of switches and manipulated to change colors and blink along with the music.

Shortly after the building opened, July 4, 1909, the process of additions and improvements was begun that would continue for the next half century. The movie theater was enclosed and enlarged to seat more than 500, and sound on the film replaced the pianist in the pit. Facilities for radio broadcasting were added and the unfinished lower level was converted into a restaurant and bar. A coffee shop was built near the rear. Roller skating, wrestling matches and antique shows were added to the activities.

Until the 1920s passenger boats from Chicago called

regularly at Saugatuck, some docking right alongside the Pavilion. Oldtimers will tell you that some hot summer evenings the boat to Chicago would glide into the dock and a deep voice would entone, "Last call for Chicago." At that signal the swains would drop their partners in mid two-step and rush for the gangplank, some jumping over the railing of the second floor balcony in their haste to climb aboard.

From 1914 until 1924 the *South American* and the *North American*, cruise ships of the Georgian Bay line, wintered alongside the building, remaining until late in the spring, somehow adding glamour to the structure. But in 1923 the company that held the insurance on the big white boats announced that they would no longer permit them to winter at the Pavilion docks. They pointed out the fire danger posed by the large wooden structure and made arrangements, in the fall of 1924, for new winter docks in Holland. As the building aged, and much of the glamour diminished, the potential of fire loomed larger. If the Big Pavilion ever caught fire, its detractors pointed out, there would be no hose big enough to put it out, and the entire town would go with it.

By the mid-1950s, although the big ballroom was only occasionally use for dancing, the cavernous hall hosted antique shows, and, in 1959, the First Annual Saugatuck Jazz Festival. For several years The Dock, the restaurant and bar on the lower level, was the only profit-making part of the operation. Small sailing and power vessels had replaced the big boats along the docks, and the entire structure was badly in need of maintenance. It was a Saugatuck tradition to paint the name of your boat on the riverside wall at the Big Pavilion, and by 1959 there were more boat names than red paint on the siding.

In the spring of 1960, however, things began looking up. Owners Herbert Shutter and John Constantine had finally decided to paint the building and, by the start of May, Shutter had contacted a painting firm in Chicago and they were waiting for warm, dry weather to begin work. Jack Repp, manager of the movie theater and sometime organist for the skaters, had arrived in town and was preparing for a new season.

On Friday, May 6, Repp awoke in his little room by the theater stage and went over to use the rest room at the nearby Village Hall because the water had not yet been turned on at the Pavilion. He went from there to the *Commercial Record* office, then located in a small brick building just east of the pie factory on Lake Street, to discuss the summer advertising plans.

At that time there were at least four places in town where the fire telephone rang: the Hotel Saugatuck (later Coral Gables), the Maplewood Hotel, Snug Harbor Shell station near the south end of Butler Street, and at the Harold Whipple house. About noon the phone rang. The call was answered by manager Vi Fox at the Hotel Saugatuck. The caller, Harold Leasure, whose small gray cottage was almost directly across the Kalamazoo River from the Pavilion, said simply that the Pavilion was on fire. Vi punched the siren button near the fire phone and called a member of the Fire Department, she is not sure now who, to report the location of the fire.

Morgan Edgcomb, who was working at the Snug Harbor Shell Station, picked up the phone and heard the call reporting the fire. He looked out at the nearby Pavilion but could see no sign of fire from his vantage point as he ran east and around the corner to the fire barn on Griffith street, just north of Culver Street, to fetch a fire truck.

After sounding the siren and giving the location of the fire, Vi ran from the Hotel Saugatuck down to the docks, and then south along the docks until she could see a line of fire on the outside of the Pavilion, from the water's edge to the roof, near the southwest tower, between the dance hall to the north, and the theater annex to the south. Aware of the danger to the Hotel Saugatuck, only a street's width from the north face of the Pavilion, she returned quickly to make prepare to defend her own building should the Pavilion fire spread.

74

Across Water Street from the Big Pavilion, the Hollyhock House restaurant was in the middle of the lunch rush. Cynthia Sorenson, niece of the owner, Mrs. Emily Lamb, was waiting tables. Workers and patrons heard the fire whistle and a few minutes later saw a fire truck pull up across the street. From their vantage point they saw smoke which seemed to be coming up from the river between the Pavilion and Coral Gables. People ran toward the river; someone said there was a boat on fire. When Cynthia looked across the street and through the windows of the Pavilion, she saw flames in the southwest corner above the stage in the ballroom.

She relayed this information to Mrs. Lamb who told her to lock the door and not let any more people into the restaurant. They told the customers who were there that they should leave because it looked like the Pavilion was on fire and their building would be in danger. "Everyone was very calm," Cynthia said, "and just sat there watching the activity." Soon a few, who had finished their meals, paid their bills and left. Some of the workers from the Harriss Pie Co., including Cynthia's sister Marjorie, who had been waiting to be served, departed. While fire trucks gathered, an elderly Saugatuck lady tried the locked door. When she received no response to her knocks, she went around to the back door demanding to be let in so she could have a piece of pie and some coffee. Mrs. Lamb told her the Big Pavilion was burning and she couldn't let any more people into the restaurant, but eventually gave her some pie to take home, just to get her to go away. By this time the flames had shot across the inside of the Pavilion and the danger was more obvious. Cynthia grabbed the money from the cash register, went through the house to get the dog, and retreated to the backyard of the Elms Hotel (later the Petter Gallery) which appeared to be out of immediate danger.

Saugatuck Fire Department records show that the first truck went out at 12:05 p.m. Later some firemen would say that they had hesitated briefly when the siren blew because it was so near noon, a time when the siren was often blown as a test.

The rear of the Pavilion ablaze as men hose down the docks.

One downtown resident, home from work for the day, heard the siren and saw the trucks leave the old station on Griffith Street from her front window. In the days before firemen carried radios the location of a fire was always written on a blackboard in the station, so that the volunteers who missed going out with the trucks could follow. On this day she crossed the street to read the location of the fire on the board. It said, "Pavilion."

Jim Boyce, a Saugatuck fireman and part-time police officer, had just sat down for lunch and had taken the first bite of his sandwich when the fire siren blew. (The next day he would find the lunch where he had left it, with just that one bite missing from the sandwich.) He headed downtown on Lake Street toward the smoke driving a 1956 Ford which was the family car, but which was also outfitted and painted to serve as a part-time police car. Just past the intersection of Butler and Culver Streets, at the rear of the Village Hall, he pulled the vehicle across the road blocking traffic to Water street from the south. "Then I just left it there," Boyce said, "with the lights blinking and the keys in the ignition."

Boyce and Saugatuck Fire Chief Bill Wilson, who owned the Gourmet Shop on Culver Street, were among the earliest arrivals. They discovered that all of the doors to the Pavilion were locked or blocked. To gain admission to the building, they kicked in the Water Street entrances to the theater, the main dance floor door at street level, and the entrance to The Dock on the lower level. There were no flames and very little smoke inside.

Convinced there was a fire someplace, they went back out to direct arriving fire equipment. Less than three minutes later when the hoses were ready to swing into action, and they had opened the north doors to the ballroom, flames were raging through the structure.

One passing motorist reported later that she saw smoke coming from the tower on the south end of the Pavilion when she drove by shortly after 12. She drove on down the street for two blocks looking for a telephone, and, by the time she returned, the whole body of the building was engulfed in flames.

The fire broke out first on the river side. Harry Newnham, the Superintendent of Public Works for the Village of Saugatuck, brought one fire truck down Mason Street between the Hotel Saugatuck and the Pavilion, to the water's edge, and pulled his truck out on the dock itself near the north end of the Pavilion, planning to draw water from the river. He looked up and saw billowing flame, 50 feet overhead, assessed the chances of the wooden dock catching fire, and beat a hasty retreat with the truck up the hill, where hoses were attached to the hydrant at Mason and Water Streets. (The next day he would discover that most of the paint had been blistered off one side of the truck.)

Edgcomb took another Saugatuck Fire Department

truck down to the water on the south end of the Pavilion, where he could draw water from the river, but hoses were still unable to reach the west side of the building, which extended over the water, being constructed on pilings driven into the river bottom.

There were several yachts tied up at Cook Park. Boyce and Bob Sergeant of the Singapore Yacht Club and others sought to move them because of the danger from flames spreading, and also to clear a path to the water for fire hoses. They had keys only for Sergeant's boat, but they untied the others and pushed them into the river where they were roped together and towed to a safe place.

At the Lloyd J. Harriss Pie Co., just down the street from the burning building, work was stopped as employes who served in the volunteer fire departments of Saugatuck and Douglas, left in response to the fire sirens. Remaining employes trooped out to see what was going on. At the end of the street the south end of the Pavilion was visible, engulfed in flames.

Saugatuck was between police chiefs and had only one deputy who was not a member of the fire department, but arriving law enforcement officers from the Michigan State Police and the Allegan County Sheriff's Department, assisted by the police chief from Fennville, moved quickly to stop traffic, except for emergency vehicles, on Lake Street leading into town, and down Water Street, although people on foot and kids on bicycles continued to rush toward the site to help or watch. At that time local and state law enforcement agencies used different radio bands. Once they had a second blockade in place, state troopers moved the Boyce car to permit easier access to the fire by arriving fire trucks, and then continued to use the vehicle to monitor the local radio and to aid in the placement of additional fire equipment.

Shortly after their arrival it was clear to the fire fighters that there was no hope of saving any of the Pavilion building and efforts were concentrated on keeping the fire from spreading. Their hoses were trained on the Hollyhock House where a Holland reporter later wrote that plates of pancakes and sausages had been left on the tables by departing customers. Mrs. Lamb's son, Frank, was away at college, but friends in town were especially concerned about his large record and book collection and came to help remove it to a place of safety. Other residents and workers in downtown Saugatuck left their posts and came to help remove furniture and equipment from the restaurant, expecting that it would be the next structure to burn. The heat was so intense that windows were exploding and, later, some plastic sugar shaker covers were found melted shut from the heat and candles on the table were bent over in inverted U-shapes.

The Douglas fire siren sounded just moments after the Saugatuck siren. Under Fire Chief Bob Wicks firemen got the larger of the Douglas trucks from the old fire barn under the Douglas Village Hall. "As we drove down the Blue Star," Wicks said, "we could see smoke just starting to rise over the building. By the time we turned at Lake Street and got around the curve it was ablaze." They parked at the south end of the Pavilion and hooked onto a fire hydrant on Water Street. Shortly afterwards they brought the second Douglas fire truck, a pumper which would suck water from the river, and set it up near the Hotel Saugatuck with three members of the department manning hoses on the roof of that building. One fireman's wife said, "I was relieved when I saw that he was away from the Big Pavilion and on the roof of the hotel until I remembered that the hotel was even older than the Pavilion."

The dining room of the Hotel Saugatuck was about to start its second summer of business under new owner Tom Johnson, a restauranteur from East Lansing. An additional dining room was being constructed south of the old one and the windows on the south side of the addition were separated by only the narrow end of Mason Street from the burning building.

(Top, the theater entrance as the flames approached, and, (bottom) the marquee crashes onto the entryway.

The new room was not yet in use, the carpet had not been installed and furniture was not in place, but the draperies had been hung. These were pulled across the windows and, as the fire grew hotter and the windows were broken by the heat, the curtains were nailed to the frames and watered down to keep sparks from coming inside. Even with the water being sprayed on it constantly, the south wall of the new dining room was too hot inside to touch.

As the fire at the Pavilion burned northward, everyone was evacuated from the Hotel Saugatuck building, although firemen and workers remained on the roof. Vi estimates that, at one point, the flames were soaring three times higher than the roof of the hotel. The north wall of the Pavilion, nearest the Hotel Saugatuck, was the last one to fall. To everyone's relief breakage in the support timbers caused the wall to fall inward, although portions came within ten feet of the Hotel walls and some stray debris actually bounced off the wall and foundation.

"It was really terrifying when the wall fell," Vi said. "Everyone I knew was on the roof and we didn't know quite what the fire would do." Although 5 p.m. was the usual opening hour for the restaurant, workers were in the building when the fire started and were able to open doors and windows giving the firemen access to various levels of the roof. Owner Tom Johnson was in the hospital, recovering from surgery, and did not know of the fire until a reporter called asking for a comment. He immediate called Vi and told her to "get the place open and get ready for the biggest night we have ever had." A clean-up crew was set to work as soon as the building could be entered, and fans were positioned to remove smoke and some of the heat. One waitress, who lived in Saugatuck and could walk to work, came in early and helped dispense coffee and refreshments to the emergency workers. Several parties had been planned for the evening and Vi cancelled those. She had a *Holland Evening Sentinel* reporter include in a brief story of the fire carried in their evening edition, a notice that all reservations for the Hotel Saugatuck restaurant for that evening had been cancelled. However, the restaurant stayed open although neither Vi nor the waitress remember that there were too many paying guests. One fireman recalls clearly stumbling by the hotel porch at 2 a.m. and being handed a sandwich, his first food since breakfast.

In addition to preventive efforts at the Hotel Saugatuck, hoses from other departments were trained on the Corner Grill, owned by the Krawitz family at the southeast corner of Mason and Water Streets (later Marro's), and the White House directly across Water Street. Special attention was also given to Flint's Store, a large multi-floor wooden structure at the southwest corner of Mason and Butler Streets. The store, even older than both the Pavilion and the Hotel Saugatuck building, towered above surrounding buildings and seemed in a direct line to be ignited by air-borne burning particles. All of downtown watched nervously. Post office workers identified equipment that should be rescued if evacuation seemed advisable, then crossed Butler street to stand on the steps of the Community Cleaners to watch the progress and direction of the flames that were clearly visible over the tops of the Butler Street businesses.

The middle of the building burned first, followed by the theater area and then the north end. Onlookers gathered near the Village Hall and on the Butler Hotel's porches. The *Holland Evening Sentinel* would primly report in its afternoon edition, "All of Saugatuck turned out for the fire, but the orderly crowd stayed well back from the blaze." There was a reason they gave the flames wide berth. One youngster, whose mother had firmly told her not to get any closer to the fire than the drug store corner remembers that, even from this distance, the heat of the fire was clearly palpable.

If the spectators were aware of the heat of the flames, the firemen were having some real problems. Two men, whose job it was to keep hoses trained on the Hollyhock House,

82

remember hosing down each other at intervals, as their clothing and bodies got uncomfortably hot. Seeing firemen trying to shield their faces with their gloved hands, one downtown business owner brought unguentine from the drug store for those exposed directly to the heat of the fire. Several firemen suffered burned hands and blistered faces, and one employee of the Hotel Saugatuck fell from the kitchen roof and was hospitalized with a back injury.

A frame from a home movie film shows the flames and smoke from the fire towering above the stores on Butler Street.

Spectators and, for a time, fire fighters, were withdrawn from the area between the Pavilion and the Hotel Saugatuck when officials feared that a power pole with a transformer was

83

in danger of burning through and dropping live wires on those below. As soon as Consumers Powers workers arrived, power was shut off to the immediate area.

At the drug store, men climbed on top of the building to wet down the flat roof with a hose to lessen the chance that a stray ember would set it on fire, then remained to stamp out sparks until the height of the fire was past. Owners and residents of homes near the fire hosed down their roofs and hung wet blankets over windows and doors to protect them from the heat.

The best view of the burning building was from across the river. Abigail De Young remembers the day clearly. Although she was a native of Saugatuck, she had lived in Iowa for some years before purchasing a summer residence here. The family had just left for the beach stopping at the old Redwood Drive-In restaurant in Douglas for a sack of hamburgers to take along for lunch. Shortly after they had arrived at the Oval beach, the Saugatuck siren blew, followed very shortly by the one from Douglas. "When the second siren went, we knew it was something big," she said. "We just piled back in the car." Smoke was billowing above the trees before they reached the end of the beach road, and they pulled out at the shoreline across from the burning building to watch. One of the towers, its base burned through, toppled into the water, and Mrs. De Young remembers people in a canoe pouring and splashing water on the burning wood, to keep it from floating too near a boat and setting another fire.

From the highway bridge motorists seeing the leaping flames were sure the entire town would go. However, even as the fire burned the wind shifted from the usual westerly to south-south east, carrying the embers away from downtown, but sending them across the lake where they threatened many summer cottages in the wooded dunes and along the river.

Theater manager and organist Repp, who followed the

smoke and fire trucks back to the Pavilion, tried to save his personal belongings, including a life-time collection of sheet music, but his little room near the stage was just below where the fire had started. In addition to the music, including two of his own compositions, he lost all his clothing and color slides of a summer in Europe. "I went over to Tara," Repp recalled later, "to call Shutter. I was there when the roof fell in."

At the Saugatuck school atop the Allegan Street hill, which, at that time, housed all the students in the entire Saugatuck system, kindergarten through high school, both the nearby Saugatuck siren and the more distant one from Douglas could be heard. Many of the students were eating lunch in the cafeteria and looked out the west window where they saw black smoke just beginning to rise above the trees. One high school senior says he was in the library when the first siren went off "and downtown less than five minutes later." At the scene he and many of his classmates assisted firemen with hoses and other equipment.

P. G. Walter left the cafeteria on his motor scooter and headed downtown. Near the drug store he was met by a policeman or fireman (he can't remember which) and was asked to go across the river and "see what's happening" over there. He sped for the bridge and down Ferry Street. When he arrived directly across the river from the Pavilion, he saw many little fires being started by floating embers, and observed that the William Underwood cottage just north of the Oval Beach road, near The Beachway, was already seriously on fire. "There were people standing around in knots but everybody was watching the fire across the river. No one was paying any attention to what was going on around them." He tried to call for help on a pay phone nearby but it was either broken or disconnected for the winter, so he remounted his motor scooter and sped back across the river.

He found a fireman downtown and described the fire at the cottage, the many small fires in the woods, and a large grass fire developing near Casa Loma Resort. While the firemen located several reels of hose, Walter went downtown and traded his scooter for a panel truck used in his father's drycleaning business. At the firehall he loaded three firemen, six or seven high school students, and several reels of fire hose in the back of the windowless truck and headed back across the bridge.

Jack Baker, high school principal, was notified of the problems across the river and asked boys from the junior and senior high school for volunteers to assist in efforts across the river. According to some sources, Baker himself drove the bus (the regular driver was a fireman) which took them to the other side of the river armed with buckets, brooms and shovels, to help stamp out grass fires, and embers which fell in the woods and on cottages west of the river. Several teachers also left school at that time to help supervise the bus load of students. With a shortage of staff, the junior high and high school girls were confined to study hall in the library where one student remembers you could only see the fire if you leaned around the corner of the room's south window.

There was a cafeteria in one end of the home economics room, but many of the children who lived in town went home for lunch. When recess was over and classes resumed, one first grade teacher took attendence and discovered that one student had failed to return. She notified the superintendent who attempted to locate him, or at least to notify his family that he was not in school. The student was eventually discovered at the fire, accompanied by his mother. There are conflicting recollections about whether the rest of the school was released early. One teacher said she didn't think it was. Her memory was that it was a very long afternoon; her pupils had "too good a view" of the flames and smoke from their classroom window. The district at that time only owned two buses, and may have had to wait until the bus returned from west of the river to have transportation for the bus riders. Whether it was on time, slightly early, or about 1 p.m. one elementary school student remembers clearly that the class was told that bus riders were to board the bus IMMEDIATELY and that the walkers (children who lived within walking distance of the school) were to GO STRAIGHT HOME.

High school teacher Edie Lambers was particularly concerned by the turn of events, because she was faculty advisor for the senior play which was scheduled to debut at 8 p.m. that evening. The play was a romantic comedy in three acts entitled, "Calm Yourself." The plot centered around the love life of an interior decorator named Harold Ainsworth. (It would open on time and a reviewer praised the young actors for their "casual aplomb.")

At the Saugatuck Woman's Club auditorium on Hoffman Street just east of Butler Street, members were gathering for the last regular meeting of the club year. Mary Ann Curtis, whose husband, the Rev. James Curtis, had been ordained from All Saints Episcopal Church, was scheduled to give a book review. The Curtises had moved to Gary, Indiana, but Mrs. Curtis returned each year in May to do a program for the Womens Club. She had been invited by Gladys Taylor, president, for a pre-meeting luncheon at the Taylor home on the river near the north end of Saugatuck. As Mrs. Curtis drove into town from the lakeshore it looked first like Douglas was on fire, but when she came out to the Blue Star Highway she could see that it was the Pavilion. As she tried to get to the Taylor house she encountered Jim Webster, producer-director at the Red Barn Theatre, the local summer playhouse. He asked her what she was doing in town and laughed when she told him of the planned program, commenting that it looked like she was being "upstaged by a fire." The leaders of the club, most of whom were attending the luncheon at the Taylor home, debated cancelling the meeting, and Mrs. Curtis told them that she felt they should because everyone would be concerned about husbands and sons fighting the fire, or the safety of their own houses, "No one would care much about a book review." They agreed and a note was put on the door of the Woman's

87

Club Auditorium postponing the meeting.

Thinking they had all afternoon, the ladies proceeded with their luncheon at a more leisurely pace, watching television coverage of the wedding of Princess Margaret in England and monitoring the progress of the fire. "We couldn't see the Pavilion from the house, but we could see debris floating down the river, some of it still burning," Mrs. Curtis said. They had not actually begun the main course of the luncheon when the phone rang and the caller told them that the front rows of the auditorium were full, and others were arriving expecting the meeting to go forward at 2 p.m. as planned. No one seemed to know what had happened to the sign on the door. Mrs. Taylor threw on her hat and gloves and headed for the club house. She promised to make the business meeting as long as possible and advised Mrs. Curtis to at least have something to eat before arriving to start the program. After a pause to compose her thoughts, and to grab a bite, the featured speaker entered the door of the auditorium just in time to hear Mrs. Taylor say, "And here comes our program now." The scheduled review was of Billie Burke's biography, "With Powder on My Nose." Mrs. Curtis said later, "I'm just glad I had planned a comedy presentation. The whole situation was absurd, and if I had tried to be serious it would have been ludicrous."

By the time the firemen, volunteers and hoses arrived on the west bank of the river, it was already too late to save the Underwood cottage, but they were able to keep that portion of the fire from spreading and to put out many other small fires that were being started by burning embers blown across the water. The roof of at least one other cottage took flame, and the students struggled to get on top of the house by crawling up the porch supports on the screened-in porch. All the ladders and other equipment that would have been helpful were packed away for the winter. The cottage was saved with only minor damage and the owners later sent the high school a large check in appreciation. Casa Loma resort on the west side of the river was also damaged by flying embers. A large burning fragment fell on the top of another cottage, once known as Allahee Lodge. Because the roof was of tin the fire did not spread, but even today when the roof is scraped for painting, the scars of the fire can be seen.

A view from across the river.

Walter said he was sent back to town for something and he left the west shore fires in the drycleaning truck. Coming around the curve near Casa Loma, he came radiator to radiator with the largest fire truck he had ever seen. It was a big flat-nosed city-style apparatus, the size of a semi-truck when viewed head-on, from either South Haven or Holland, that had been sent to aid efforts on that side of the river. He estimates that at one time there were four or five trucks on the west bank of the river. When the fire in town was under control, additional hose was brought over and run into the woods at Minister's Path.

Irving Tucker, whose parents owned a cottage in the Oak Knoll subdivision near the Oval Beach road, was working at Bohn Aluminum in South Haven when a Douglas woman checked in for work about 3:15 and mentioned the big fire going on in Saugatuck. Without pause he headed north and by the time he hit M-89 could see smoke billowing above the trees. Ferry Street was blocked by fire trucks filling their watertanks at a hydrant near Campbell Road, but they let him pass when he said he was a home owner. When he got to the first clear view across the river, about at Casa Loma, he could see the burning Pavilion and all the fire apparatus pumping water into the structure and onto the roofs of nearby buildings. As the roof timbers collapsed, the tar paper on the rounded roof billowed out from the heat and smoke and was caught by the wind. Pieces of it floated across the river "like kites" and came down in the woods from Casa Loma to about Mount Baldhead and inland to Camp Gray. The tar paper, thick from many reapplications over the years, stayed hot and started many small fires in the underbrush until the woods on the west side of the river were full of smoke. The Oak Knoll subdivision was south of the Oval Beach road some distance west of the river. Most of the buildings are located behind the row of cottages which front on the road and are hidden from view behind a wooded dune. Tucker and Henry Barber of Allegan, another cottage owner, beat out fires in the small summer community and into the woods all afternoon and into the night. One of Tucker's strongest memories was a feeling of isolation. There seemed to be no one else around and he has no memories of seeing any fire trucks west of the river except for those filling their tanks at the Campbell Road hydrant.

Although they probably heard the siren, many townspeople did not realize the location and scope of the disaster until school children began arriving home with tales of student volunteers, fire trucks and the smoke and flame they could see from the schoolhouse hill. One Saugatuck mother said she then took her three school-aged children and her two pre-schoolers down to view the fire from a safe distance. "I felt it was an historic day in our town. Something they should see and remember."

Calls went out to nearby fire departments for assistance. Additional trucks were sent from Douglas, Bangor, Graafschap, South Haven, Ganges, Allegan Township, Allegan City, Holland, Bloomingdale and two Clyde-Manlius Township trucks operated by the Fennville Fire Department. There was also a Civil Defense four wheel drive vehicle from the Conservation Department. In all there were 16 vehicles, mostly pumpers and tankers, on the scene. No area department at that time owned an aerial truck. It was estimated that at one point in the effort, 24 streams of water were playing simultaneously on the burning Pavilion, and structures endangered nearby. When a truck leaves its own fire station, the department in the next town is alerted to be prepared in case a fire occurs while the the equipment is out of town. The day the Pavilion burned the possibility that additional equipment might be needed in Saugatuck if the fire spread, caused an alert across lower Michigan that reached as far as Detroit.

Also assisting with the task were two United States Air Force enlisted men who were stationed at the radar installation on the top of Mount Baldhead. According to the next week's newspaper the two, "did yeoman service throughout the afternoon and evening, interrupted only once when one had to return to the radar station for a while."

The major part of the fire was over in an hour. By late afternoon nothing was left of the structure but a corner of the hot dog stand in the southeast end of the ground floor and the charred outline of the base of the northeast tower. The cables which had spanned the ballroom were recognizable, twisted by the heat. In the northeast corner where roller skates were stored and rented during skating season, the shelves had burned through and there was a pile of blackened metal clamp-on skates amid the smoking debris. In the basement restaurant were lumps of melted glass, all that was left of hundreds of bar room glasses and thousands of lightbulbs.

One Holland resident who heard of the fire on the radio and drove south with two high school buddies said they saw the smoke from the Holland road, but all that he remembers remaining were smoking pilings which had formed the foundation for the wooden building. Another Holland man who had spent many happy hours on the dance floor remembers most vividly the empty feeling when he rounded the curve of Culver Street, and instead of the looming shape of the Big Pavilion saw only sky, river and ashes.

Later summer visitors who were in Chicago during the fire would claim that from the upper floors of some of the buildings in the Loop you could see the smoke and flames of the fire, between noon and 1 p.m., during the height of activity.

Saugatuck firemen who worked out of town saw smoke rising in the sky and went directly to the scene, taking over from their colleagues who had been on duty with no break since noon. Saugatuck Fire Department records show that most firemen that day were credited with 12 hours of duty, and three worked 21 hours. Hoses poured water on the ashes all night, and the embers were fully out and watersoaked by morning.

Reports of the fire were carried in area daily newspapers on Friday, with additional stories and pictures on Saturday. Several Douglas cottagers called anxiously after reading a Friday *South Haven Daily Tribune* with a late bulletin headlined, "Huge Fire Theatens Saugatuck." The short story carried the news that, "Wind-whipped flames today engulfed the Big Pavilion and flying embers touched off grass and woods fires across the Kalamazoo River in Douglas." The misunderstanding occurred because the reporter was unfamiliar with Douglas and Saugatuck boundary lines. Virtually all of the fires west of the river occured north of Campbell Road, within Saugatuck village limits.

Saturday and Sunday traffic was bumper-to-bumper from both directions. At one time the line of cars from the north extended the length of Water Street and east to Holland Street, crawling along to see what Saugatuck was like without the Big Pavilion. Few had a good look at the ruins because most of the debris was below street level. Stores which had already received the season's stock of post cards did a brisk business in views of the Big Pavilion, many mailed to out-of-town relatives and friends spreading the news. More thant 30 years later post card views of the Big Pavilion are still a big seller in Saugatuck post card shops.

Despite persistent rumors that the fire was intentionally set, some unsubstantiated, some from those who profess to have inside information, Sgt. Walter Burns, fire marshal for southern Michigan working out of the Paw Paw State Police post, filed a report that "arson was not suspected." In an interview he said that the origins of the fire "could not be determined." It had begun near the southwest tower, possibly in one of three small rooms located above the theatre screen. (These rooms were sometimes used as temporary lodging by various employees and musicians, but there was no one occupying them at the time of the fire. The most unusual feature of the rooms was the rope for the stage curtain which ran in one side and out the other.) Burns said the center section of the building burned first, followed by the north end, with the theater going last and burning somewhat slower because there was more in the room to burn. He was uncertain whether problems with a nearby electrical transformer that had occurred earlier in the week had any connection with the fire. The sergeant reported that the spread of the flames may have been aided by a central flue in the air conditioning unit. Because the electricity had just been turned on for the season and because the first flame seen outside of the structure ran straight up and down, some speculated that old insulation removed from electrical wires by birds, or mice, or squirrels during the winter, had caused a short and sparked the blaze.

The Commercial Record

VOLUME NINETY-TWO   10 CENTS   SAUGATUCK, MICHIGAN, FRIDAY, MAY 18, 1980   NUMBER TWENTY

New Building To Replace Pavilion

FLAMES DESTROY BIG PAVILION IN ONLY 45 MINUTES

Fire of an undetermined origin swept through the Big Pavilion shortly after noon last Friday and within 45 minutes had reduced the huge vacation center into a broad pile of debris and twisted iron.

Firemen from the surrounding area helped the Saugatuck Fire Department keep it contained, and with heroic effort by many it was kept from spanning the narrow street to the Hotel Saugatuck and buildings on the opposite side of Water street.

A mild breeze from the south-southeast carried embers away from the village, landing them in the wooded hills across the Kalamazoo and starting innumerable small fires that were quickly put out. One building, the cottage of William Underwood of Chicago, on the first hill of the Oval road, burned.

Flames Have Start

The fire started in the vicinity of the southwest corner of the second-floor ballroom and was first noticed by people on the other side of the river. Fire Chief Bill Wilson and others with him found no blaze on the ground floor after they had broken through the north door to the Dock.

By the time they were outside to get equipment into action the flames had started raging through the large structure. Unable to attack it from the water side, firemen tried to fight a delaying action from Water street and the ends.

Fire Kept Contained

Equipment from surrounding communities had come to aid the Saugatuck and Douglas Departments, and streams from all land sides were played on the inferno. Immediate attention was given to saving Hotel Saugatuck, the restaurants of Mrs. Emily Lamb and Roy Krawitz.

Broken windows and blistered walls were the main damages to the nearby buildings. The north wall was last to go and breakage in the support timbers kept the wall from falling on the Hotel Saugatuck.

From then on, it was a matter of putting out the embers in the debris. Streams were kept on it through the night and the smoldering timbers were soaked by morning. From then on, the remains of the Big Pavilion was something for sightseers.

INSIDE STUFF

After you have finished reading of the fire, look at the inside pages for more news. You'll find:

Aldrich informs employers of teenagers on permits.

Maycroft appointed chief of police.

Gilman awarded Silver Beaver Conservation Department may rule on trawlers this week.

And many, many other interesting stories.

To yachtsmen this scene meant Saugatuck, and to motorists across the river it was probably the most familiar sight. The picture dramatically shows the nearness of the Hotel Saugatuck to the Pavilion and emphasizes the great work done by firemen and citizens in halting the spread of the fire.
(Photo by Bill Simmons)

The Day the Pavilion Burned

"THANK GOD, IT'S OVER"

"Thank God! It's happened. It's over."

This quotation was echoed in various forms by scores of the residents of Saugatuck. For years the Big Pavilion had been a dreaded threat. A fire and a southwest wind would wipe out the greater part of the village. When it came the wind was from the SSE, carried embers away from the village. And, fire fighters valiantly contained the fire to its area.

AID FROM CIVIL DEFENSE

Dave Weston, head of the Allegan County Civil Defense, has informed Lynn McCray, area director, that that organization will pick up the tab for coffee and food served the weary firemen, that gas tanks of all fire trucks were to be filled at CD expense. The rescue truck was sent here from Allegan and stood by for any emergency.

Fruitless Plans

In Chicago on Monday before the fire, Herbert Shutter had contracted with a painting firm to come here and give the big red building a new coat of paint. On Wednesday night he had engaged two waitresses. Jack Repp, who was to have run the theatre, had booked his films for the summer and ordered advertising material.

People Make News

When Lucile Weiter saw firemen shielding their faces from the terrific heat she hied to the drug store, got all of the unguentine in stock, went to the fire and passed it out.

The cruiser, Lara Jane, is tied up back of the Hotel Saugatuck annex. When Julie Dorn tried to get back of the hotel for a better look, the skipper barred the way brandishing a wicked looking boathook. He stopped her but not until after she had delivered a stiff reprimand.

Mrs. Garth Wilson phoned her husband at his work in Holland. In less than 30 minutes he had on his firemen's helmet and was at work.

Miss Jessie Veits, ever thoughtful, busied herself making fresh hot coffee and carrying it down the street to firemen.

Ready for Flight

Many residents near the Pavilion prepared for flight, some even removing their valuables and cherished possessions as a precaution. Had the wind been from the southwest and stronger, few would have had time to stop for anything before fleeing.

The Coffee Shop corner was still standing as flames were racing toward the north end of the building. After the walls and roof had fallen, all that remained was part of the hot dog stand, the southeast corner of the once lofty structure.
(Photo by Dale Ro...)

The ruins of the Big Pavilion were still smoldering when Herbert E. Shutter and John Constantine, owners, were starting plans for a new building, with an opening date set for July 4th in 1961, but 1960.

In a large room in the Hotel Saugatuck, overlooking the debris of the onetime vacation center they worked with Takeo Ito Peoria Ill, a keen, sharp-thinking architect who is a graduate of the University of Oklahoma.

They sketched out a floor plan of approximately 125 by 260 feet, with the length paralleling Kalamazoo Lake. In the northeast corner of the site they located a new movie theater which will seat 500 people.

Include Dance Floor

The length of the water front would have tables for dancing a the cocktail lounge. An area for the kitchen, toilets, storerooms and utility rooms had the choice of two different locations.

The main entrance would be down a broad stairway from Water street. On entering, the theatre entrance would be at the left. Two other entrances were set on the north and south ends of the building.

Slips for Boats

Between the building and water's edge would be a crosswalk nine feet wide. Instead the old parallel docking cruisers and yachts, slips are being planned with catwalks between caring for 20-24 boats. Old piers, burned to the water's edge, would be made usable by capping.

Shutter returned to Chicago Sunday afternoon and Ito to Peoria. Constantine, who has a Chicago Wednesday and the firm expect to confer on the new plan. Meantime, Ralph Trau has contract to clear the site of debris and started the first of the week.

94

Saturday owners Shutter and Constantine, and manager H. A. McDonald gathered to inventory the lost contents of the building. In addition to some of McDonald's best work as an amateur photographer which was hanging on his office walls they listed five pianos (four grand pianos and one upright), 400 pairs of roller skates, a new Cinemascope movie screen, and an air conditioner. Shutter lost three oil paintings of the Big Pavilion and four pieces of furniture from his Illinois home which had been reupholstered in Michigan and which he had put off taking home with him until it was too late.

The *Commercial Record* which was published the day of the fire, having been printed the day before, was too late to record the event. By the May 16 edition there was not much the local paper could add to the story of the fire; instead the *Record* headlined a hopeful bit of news. While the Pavilion still smoldered, owners Shutter and Constantine had met with an architect to design a new vacation center to replace the burned out structure. They sketched a floor plan of 125 by 260 feet, with a new movie theater in one corner, and a dining and cocktail lounge. But the cost of construction far exceeded original estimates and available funds and the project was abandoned. The movie theater moved to the old high school gymnasium, but the atmosphere was different and shortly after the plans for the new building were cancelled, the theater manager Jack Repp also threw in the towel.

Ralph Troutman received the contract for cleaning up the debris and he separated the copper wire and later the iron for salvage. Looking around for a dumping ground for ashes, melted glass, and other debris, he asked Erv Kasten Sr., for permission to use a depression in the land behind the soda pop factory on 66th street. Kasten said OK and went away for the weekend. When he returned, the valley had disappeared.

The property, including the liquor license, was purchased by the Hotel Butler. Gradually, evidence of the massive structure is being obliterated. High water in the 1980s flooded the base of the old building which had been used as a parking lot by Singapore Yacht Club members, and tons of earth were brought in to raise the level of the land. An old lamppost just south of the building was removed about 1982. In 1992 all that remains to mark the site is a portion of the cement base and entrance to the movie theater on the Water Street side and that is seriously crumbling.

Some residents say the fire changed the entire atmosphere of Saugatuck. "It was an integral part of the village," one noted. "After the Pavilion was gone the bars and drinking gained in importance as a leisure time activity."

In 1959 the "First Annual" Saugatuck jazz festival had been held at the Big Pavilion. Several weeks after the fire a tongue-in-cheek sign appeared among the remaining ashes reminding people that "Last year on this site was held what was obviously the hottest jazz festival in the country . . ." The "Second Annual" festival was advertised on the sign, along with directions for purchasing tickets and reaching the new site. The festival was held at the old speedway property south of Douglas, but was not well-received. There was no "Third Annual" event.

When the Pavilion burned the feeling was best reflected in a story datelined Saugatuck, that ran May 7, 1960, on the UPI newswire. It began, "A lot of the fun in this southern Lake Michigan resort community was gone today . . ."

96